2005 Annual Report

*Migratory Bird
Conservation Commission*

Revised March 2006

I0440599

The Migratory Bird Conservation Commission

Section 2 of the Migratory Bird Conservation Act of February 18, 1929 (Act), as amended, established the Migratory Bird Conservation Commission.

Section 2. A Commission to be known as the Migratory Bird Conservation Commission, consisting of the Secretary of the Interior, as Chairman; the Administrator of the Environmental Protection Agency; the Secretary of Agriculture; two Members of the Senate, to be selected by the President of the Senate; and two Members of the House of Representatives, to be selected by the Speaker, is created and authorized to consider and pass upon any area of land, water, or land and water that may be recommended by the Secretary of the Interior for purchase or rental under this Act and to fix the price or prices at which such area may be purchased or rented; and no purchase or rental shall be made of any such area until it has been duly approved for purchase or rental by said Commission.

Any Member of the House of Representatives who is a member of the Commission, if reelected to the succeeding Congress, may serve on the Commission notwithstanding the expiration of a Congress. Any vacancy on the Commission shall be filled in the same manner as the original appointment. The ranking officer of the branch or department of a State to which is committed the administration of its game laws, or his authorized representative, shall be a member ex officio of said Commission for the purpose of considering and voting on all questions relating to the acquisition, under said sections, of areas in his State. For purposes of said sections, the purchase or rental of any area of land, water, or land and water includes the purchase or rental of any interest in any such area of land, water, or land and water.

Membership

Hon. Gale Norton
Secretary of the Interior, Chairman

Hon. Mike Johanns
Secretary of Agriculture

Hon. Stephen L. Johnson
Administrator, Environmental Protection Agency

Hon. Blanche L. Lincoln
Senator from Arkansas

Hon. Thad Cochran
Senator from Mississippi

Hon. John D. Dingell
Representative from Michigan

Hon. Curt Weldon
Representative from Pennsylvania

A. Eric Alvarez
Secretary to the Commission
Telephone: 703/358 1716

Report of the Migratory Bird Conservation Commission for the Fiscal Year 2005

*Front Cover: 2005-2006 Duck Stamp Artwork—Hooded Merganser
(Painting by Mark Anderson)*

Approvals During Fiscal Year 2005

In Fiscal Year 2005, the Migratory Bird Conservation Commission approved the acquisition boundary at one national wildlife refuge. The refuge, totaling 5,854 acres, is the Black Bayou Lake NWR in Ouachita Parish, Louisiana. The refuge was established June 16, 1997, under authority of the Emergency Wetlands Resources act of 1986. The Commission approved boundary additions, totaling 45,564 acres, to eight refuges that were previously approved by the Commission. The Commission also approved the purchase price of 7,616 acres at twelve refuges and reappproved the price at one refuge consisting of 502 acres.

Area Approvals—New Areas

State	Area	New Area Acres
Louisiana	Black Bayou Lake NWR	5,854
Total		**5,854**

Area Approvals—Additions

State	Area	Addition Acres
Arkansas	Cache River NWR	9,864
Louisiana	Bayou Cocodrie NWR	5,000
Louisiana	Red River NRW	23,686
Mississippi	Panther Swamp NWR	4,175
New Hampshire	Silvio O. Conte NF&WR	825
Texas	San Bernard NWR	1,278
Texas	Trinity River NWR	101
Virginia	Rappahannock River NWR	355
Total		**45,564**

Price Approvals

State	Area	Price Approval Acres
Louisiana	Bayou Cocodrie NWR	1,150
Louisiana	Black Bayou Lake NWR	615
Louisiana	Catahoula NWR	80
Louisiana	Cat Island NWR	160
Louisiana	Red River NWR	1,732
Louisiana	Panther Swamp NWR	702
New Hampshire	Silvio O. Conte NF&WR	516
New Jersey	Cape May NWR	191
Tennessee	Chicksaw NWR	56
Texas	San Bernard NWR	1,228
Texas	Trinity River NWR	431
Virginia	Rappahannock River NWR	355
Total		**7,616**

Price Reapprovals

State	Area	Price Reapproval Acres
Mississippi	St. Catherine Creek	502
Total		**502**

The Migratory Bird Conservation Fund

The Migratory Bird Conservation Fund provides the Department of the Interior with monies to acquire migratory bird habitat. There are three major sources of money for the Fund. The most well-known source is the revenue received from the sale of Migratory Bird Hunting and Conservation Stamps, commonly known as Duck Stamps, as provided for under the Migratory Bird Hunting and Conservation Stamp Act of March 18, 1934, as amended. The other two major sources include appropriations authorized by the Wetlands Loan Act of October 4, 1961, as amended and import duties collected on arms and ammunition. The Fund is further supplemented by receipts from the sale of products from refuge lands and rights-of-ways across national wildlife refuges, the disposal of refuge lands, and reverted Federal Aid funds.

Two land acquisition programs are financed from the Migratory Bird Conservation Fund. The first purchases major areas for migratory birds under the authority of the Migratory Bird Conservation Act. Lands acquired through this program are considered and approved by the Migratory Bird Conservation Commission. The second program acquires small natural wetlands and associated uplands located mainly in the Prairie Pothole Region of the upper Midwest. These lands, known as Waterfowl Production Areas, are acquired under the authority of the Migratory Bird Hunting and Conservation Stamp Act and do not require approval from the Commission.

During Fiscal Year 2005, the Department of the Interior obligated a total of $10,592,989 for the acquisition of land and interests in land totaling 15,097 acres in major migratory bird conservation areas. An additional $20,881,404 was obligated for projects in Waterfowl Production Areas totaling 62,148 acres.

A total of $43,484,621 was available for obligation from the Migratory Bird Conservation Fund during Fiscal Year 2005. Obligations for all Migratory Bird Conservation Fund land acquisition functions during the fiscal year totaled $43,387,007 (of which $201,815 was from prior year recoveries). Obligations equal 100 percent of the available funds.

Summary of FY 2005
MBCF Land Acquisitions
Land Contracted for Purchase or Lease

National Wildlife Refuges: Purchase

State	Area	Acres
Arkansas	Cache River	1,800
California	Grasslands WMA (easements)	1,394
California	North Central Valley WMA (easements)	449
Louisiana	Bayou Cocodrie	1,550
Louisiana	Black Bayou Lake	89
Louisiana	Cat Island	160
Louisiana	Catahoula	80
Louisiana	Red River	1,732
Maine	Rachel Carson	35
New Hampshire	Lake Umbagog	250
New Hampshire	Silvio O. Conte	499
New Jersey	Edwin B. Forsythe	69
New York	Wallkill River	45
Tennessee	Chickasaw	57
Texas	San Bernard	1,031
Texas	Trinity River	463
Virginia	Rappahannock River	117
Total		**9,820**

National Wildlife Refuges: Lease

State	Area	Acres
Colorado	Browns Park	636
Louisiana	Lacassine	640
Louisiana	Upper Ouachita	3,235
Mississippi	Dahomey	260
Mississippi	Panther Swamp	640
Mississippi	St. Catherine Creek	502
Montana	Lost Trail	240
Utah	Ouray	2,693
Wyoming	Cokeville Meadows	787
Total		**9,633**

Waterfowl Production Areas

State	Types of Acquisition	Acres
Iowa	Fee	774
Minnesota	Fee	1,772
Minnesota	Easement	2,575
Montana	Easement	5,340
Montana	Lease	1,400
North Dakota	Easement	8,645
South Dakota	Fee	960
South Dakota	Easement	35,933
Wisconsin	Fee	391
Total		**57,790**
Grand Total		**77,243**

New National Wildlife Refuge Boundary Approvals

In Fiscal Year 2005, the Migratory Bird Conservation Commission approved the acquisition boundary of one new refuge, Black Bayou Lake National Wildlife Refuge in Ouachita Parish, Louisiana. The Commission also approved the acquisition boundary of eight national wildlife refuges that were previously established: Bayou Cocodrie National Wildlife Refuge in Concordia Parish, Louisiana; Cache River National Wildlife Refuge in Jackson, Prairie,Woodruff, and Monroe Counties, Arkansas; Panther Swamp National Wildlife Refuge in Yazoo County, Mississippi; Rappahannock River Valley National Wildlife Refuge in Essex and Richmond Counties, Virginia; Red River National Wildlife Refuge in Caddo, Bossier, Desoto, Red River, and Natchitoches Parishes, Louisiana; San Bernard National Wildlife Refuge in Brazoria County, Texas; Silvio O. Conte National Fish and Wildlife Refuge, in Coos County, New Hampshire and, Trinity River National Wildlife Refuge in Liberty County, Texas.

**Black Bayou Lake
National Wildlife Refuge**
Ouachita Parish, Louisiana

Black Bayou Lake National Wildlife
Refuge was established on June 16, 1997,
under authority of the Emergency
Wetlands Resources act of 1986. To date,
3,906 acres have been acquired at this
refuge. Approximately 1,333 acres
remain to be acquired within the refuge
boundary.

The refuge consists of pristine wetlands
associated with a 2,000-acre, shallow,
cypress-studded lake, riparian areas, and
reforested cropland. The refuge has been
traditionally used by migratory and
resident waterfowl. The lake and
adjacent wetlands are vital as wintering

habitat for migratory waterfowl,
primarily mallard, pintail, redhead,
canvasback and scaup. The extensive
stands of buttonbush, cypress and tupelo
trees provide ideal breeding and brood-
rearing habitat for resident wood duck.
Black ducks and mottled ducks, which
are less common, also utilize the refuge.
This project is important to ensure
protection of this habitat as well as
restore additional habitat. The lands will
be managed for these priority species as
well as for other species as part of the
National Wildlife Refuge System.

The Commission approved the 5,854 acre
refuge boundary and also gave price
approval for a 615 acre tract on March
16, 2005.

Black Bayou Lake National Wildlife Refuge
Ouachita Parish, Louisiana

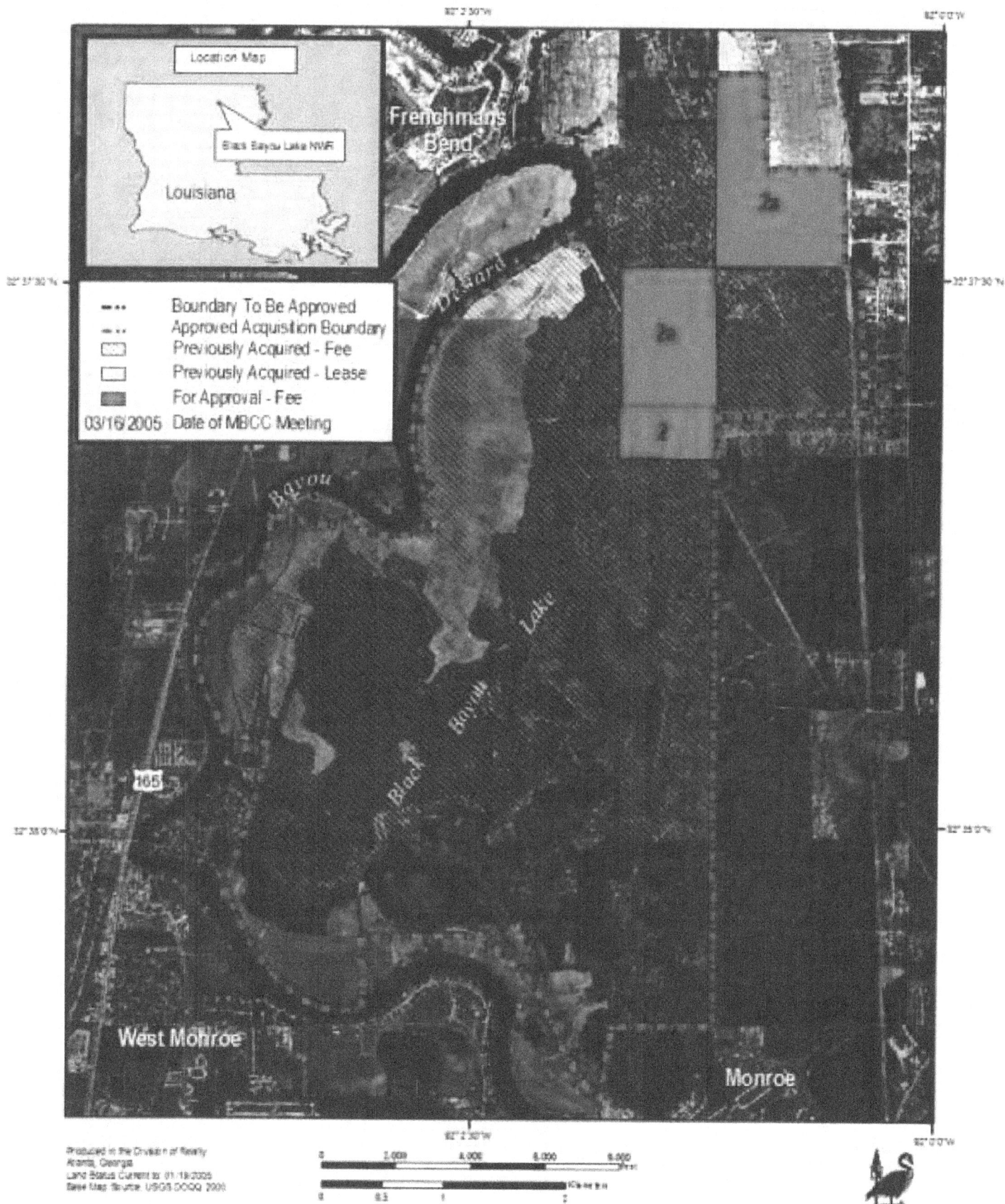

Bayou Cocodrie National Wildlife Refuge
Concordia Parish, Louisiana

The Bayou Cocodrie National Wildlife Refuge is located in Concordia Parish, Louisiana. The refuge was established on May 20, 1992, with an establishment acreage of 18,197 acres. Land and Water Conservation Act Funding was used over a three year period to acquire 9,996 acres (the largest single ownership in the refuge), from The Nature Conservancy. In 1999 the boundary was expanded and now totals 23,192 acres. Historically, the entire region was forested with bottomland hardwoods and currently includes a combination of converted wetlands. Currently of the area under protection, approximately 350 acres, consists of moist soil impoundment, that were previously cleared for agricultural use. The remainder of the acreage has been reforested. There are 22 ownerships comprising 59 percent of the refuge remaining to be acquired. Once the Hoover Slough tract is acquired 66 percent of the area within the approved acquisition boundary will be federally protected.

There are approximately 200 species of migratory birds that us the Bayou Cocodrie NWR during the year. Because of previous forest management practices, the Hoover Slough tract will provide better wintering and breeding habitat for migratory waterfowl such as the mallard, Gadwall, greenwinged teal, bluewinged teal, and neotropical migrant bird species, that are in decline such as the American woodcock, wood thrush and possibly the swallowtailed kite. It will also provide significant nesting habitat for the wood duck, hooded merganser and the great blue heron. The most distinguishing feature that sets this tract apart from current refuge property is the fact that this area has a lower and flatter elevation and holds more surface water during the winter and therefore will provide more habitat for the wintering waterfowl than the rest of the refuge, this is an important feature for the management objectives for this refuge.

The Commission approved the 5,000 acre refuge boundary addition and also gave price approval for a 1,550 acre tract on September 21, 2005.

Bayou Cocodrie National Wildlife Refuge
Concordia Parish, Louisiana

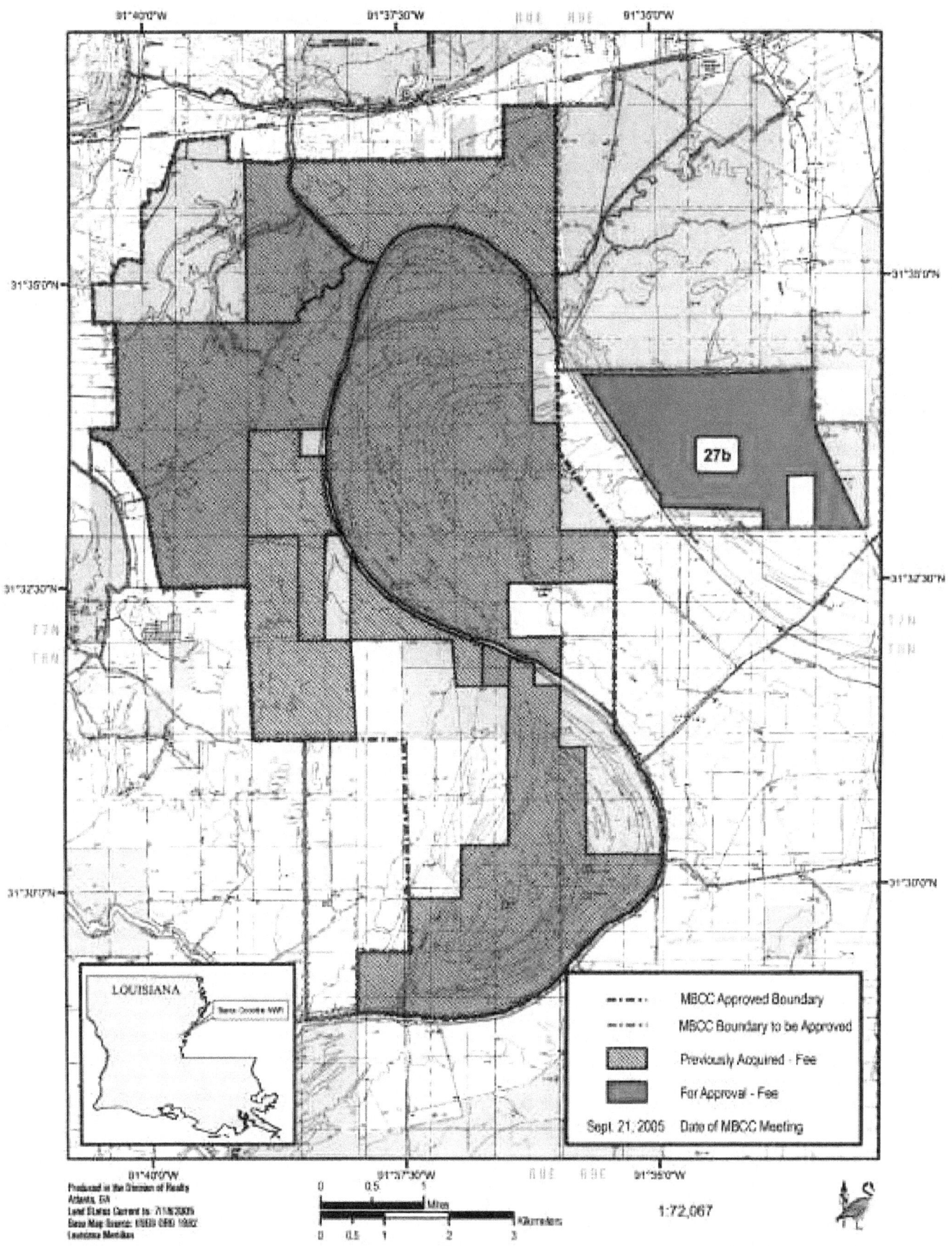

LOUISIANA

27b

MBCC Approved Boundary

MBCC Boundary to be Approved

Previously Acquired - Fee

For Approval - Fee

Sept. 21, 2005   Date of MBCC Meeting

1:72,067

Cache River National Wildlife Refuge
*Jackson, Prairie, Woodruff, and Monroe
Counties, Arkansas*

Cache River National Wildlife Refuge
was established on June 16, 1986, under
the authority of the Fish and Wildlife Act
of 1956, the Migratory Bird Conservation
Act, and the Emergency Wetlands
Resources Act of 1986. The original
refuge proposal covered 35,000 acres.
By 1998, two major expansions increased
the acquisition boundary to 175,300 acres,
which represents the 10 year floodplain
of the Cache River. Two minor expansions
since that time have brought the total
approved acquisition boundary to 185,574
acres. Within that boundary the Arkansas
Game and Fish Commission owns and
manages two Wildlife Management Areas
(WMA): Black Swamp WMA (5,967
acres), and Dagmar WMA (7,896 acres).
The State's management of the WMAs
complements the Service's management
of the refuge; therefore there are no
plans for federal acquisition or
management of the state lands. To date,
61,456 acres have been acquired using the
Land and Water Conservation Fund,
Migratory Bird Conservation Fund,
NAWCC grants, donation and transfer
of primary jurisdiction from another
Federal agency.

Cache River NWR encompasses some of
the largest remaining contiguous blocks
of bottomland hardwood forest in the
Lower Mississippi Valley, and some of the
largest remaining expanses of forested
wetlands on any tributary within the
Mississippi Alluvial Valley. With at least
twenty-four species of waterfowl utilizing
the Lower Mississippi Valley during
winter migration, this area supports one
of the largest concentrations of mallards
anywhere in North America during this
time period. It is considered by most to
be the single most important wintering
area for mallards in North America, and
some of the most important for pintails,
teal, Canada geese, and other migratory
waterfowl. The recent rediscovery on the
refuge of the Ivorybilled woodpecker, a
bird long thought extinct, highlights the
benefits that these crucial waterfowl
habitats provide to other species as well.

The purpose of this proposal is to align
the Migratory Bird Conservation
Commission's approved boundary with
the existing refuge boundary. The
Commission approved the 9,864 acre
refuge boundary addition on June 21,
2005.

Cache River National Wildlife Refuge
Jackson, Prairie, Woodruff, and Monroe Counties, Arkansas

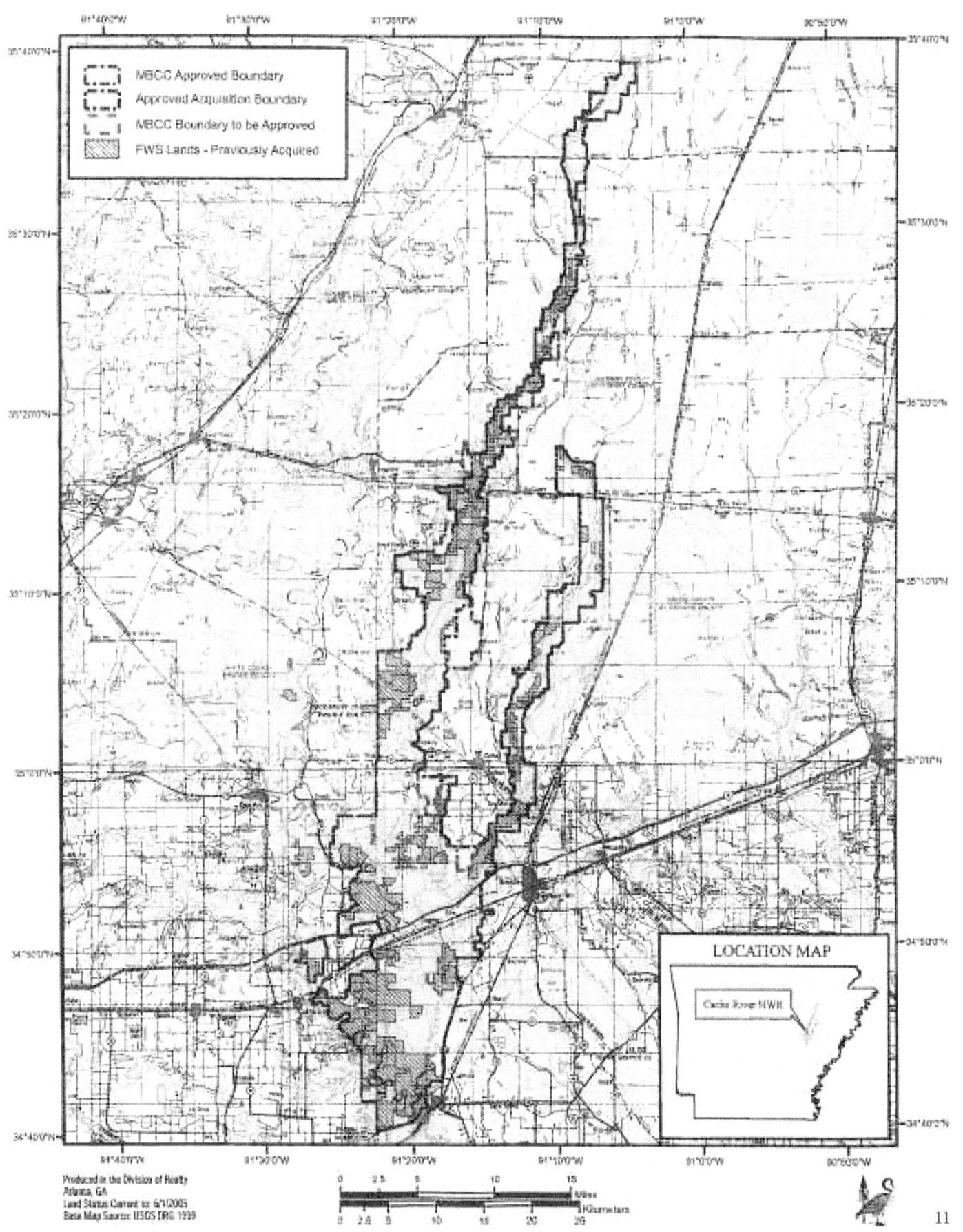

LOCATION MAP

Cache River NWR

MBCC Approved Boundary

Approved Acquisition Boundary

MBCC Boundary to be Approved

FWS Lands – Previously Acquired

Produced in the Division of Realty
Atlanta, GA
Land Status Current to: 6/1/2005
Base Map Source: USGS DRG 1999

Panther Swamp National Wildlife Refuge
Yazoo County, Mississippi

Panther Swamp National Wildlife Refuge was established under the authorities of the Migratory Bird Conservation Act (16 U.S.C. ß 715d), for use as an inviolate sanctuary, or for any other management purpose, for migratory birds; and, the Refuge Recreation Act (16 U.S.C. ß 460k1), for (1) incidental fish and wildlife-oriented recreational development, (2) the protection of natural resources, and (3) the conservation of endangered or threatened species. The initial refuge boundary was approved by the Migratory Bird Conservation Commission on September 20, 1977. An addition of 2,970 acres was approved by the Commission on July 22, 1986. On December 3, 2004, the refuge boundary was expanded by 4,175 acres bringing the total acreage in the approved acquisition boundary to 45,927 acres. To date, 27,560 acres have been acquired in fee title, 7,070 acres are managed under a cooperative agreement with the U.S. Army Corps of Engineers and 640 acres are leased from the Yazoo County School Board.

The refuge is a complex of bottomland hardwood forest, cypress swamps, seasonal and permanent wetlands, and cropland. The seasonally flooded bottomland hardwoods and other wetlands provide excellent habitat for wintering waterfowl. The more permanently flooded wetlands also provide brood habitat for locally produced wood ducks. The current average peak population for migratory waterfowl is 80,000 birds with an anticipated average peak of 150,000. A heron rookery, know as the Whites Lane Rookery, is located near the northern boundary of the property in this proposal. This rookery is a listed heritage site in the Mississippi Natural Heritage database developed by the Mississippi Department of Wildlife, Fisheries and Parks. This project is important to ensure protection of these habitats as well as restore additional habitat. Acquisition of this property would also provide access to this part of the refuge from a paved highway.

The Commission approved the 4,175 acre refuge boundary addition and price approval for a 702 acre tract on September 21, 2005.

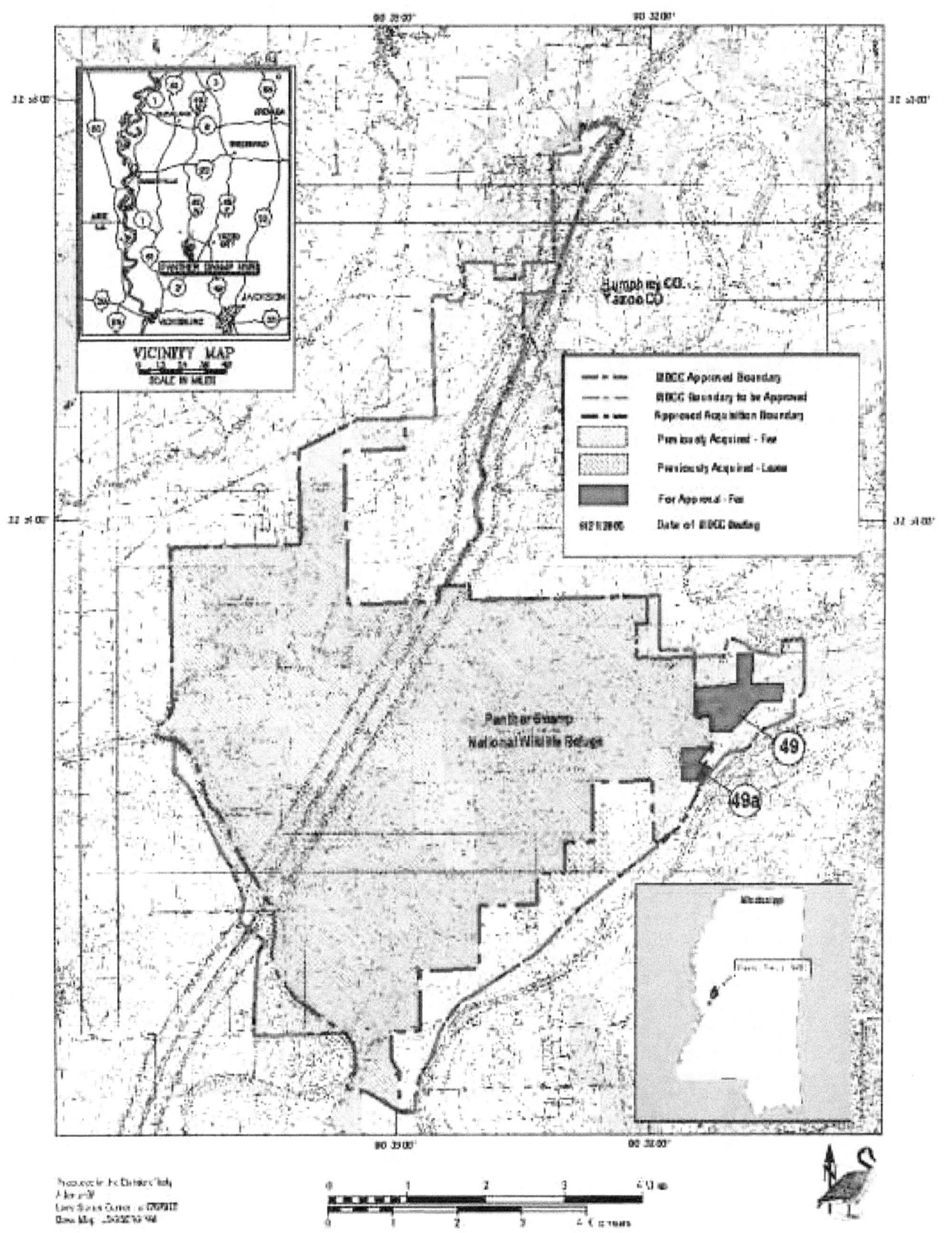

**Rappahannock River Valley
National Wildlife Refuge**
Essex and Richmond Counties, Virginia

Rappahannock River Valley National
Wildlife Refuge was established in 1996
to assist in meeting waterfowl population,
endangered species, and wetland goals of
the North American Waterfowl
Management Plan, the Service's
Chesapeake Bay/Susquehanna River
Watershed Program, and other national
and regional resource priorities. With
land purchases using both Land and
Water Conservation Act Funds,
Migratory Bird Conservation Act funds
and donations, its current area consists of
7,382 acres.

Rappahannock River and its adjacent
marshes and waters are one of the
Chesapeake Bay's most important and
productive estuarine assets, supporting a
wide diversity of subaquatic and
emergent wetland plant communities.
These lands and waters, in turn, provide
optimum habitat for large concentrations
of waterfowl and other migratory birds.
As the fourth largest river system
entering the Chesapeake Bay, the
Rappahannock River provides essential
habitat for a great diversity of migratory
birds, and for endangered and threatened
wildlife and plant species. The River has
long been recognized as one of the most
important waterfowl migration and
wintering areas in Virginia. The marshes
along the River and its tributaries have
been identified as important black duck
habitat in the Service's Category Plan for
the Preservation of black duck wintering
habitat on the Atlantic Coast. Besides
black ducks, the River supports
populations of mallards, ruddy ducks,
ringnecked ducks, canvasbacks, Canada
geese and tundra swans.

The Commission approved the 355-acre
refuge boundary addition and price
approval on June 21, 2005.

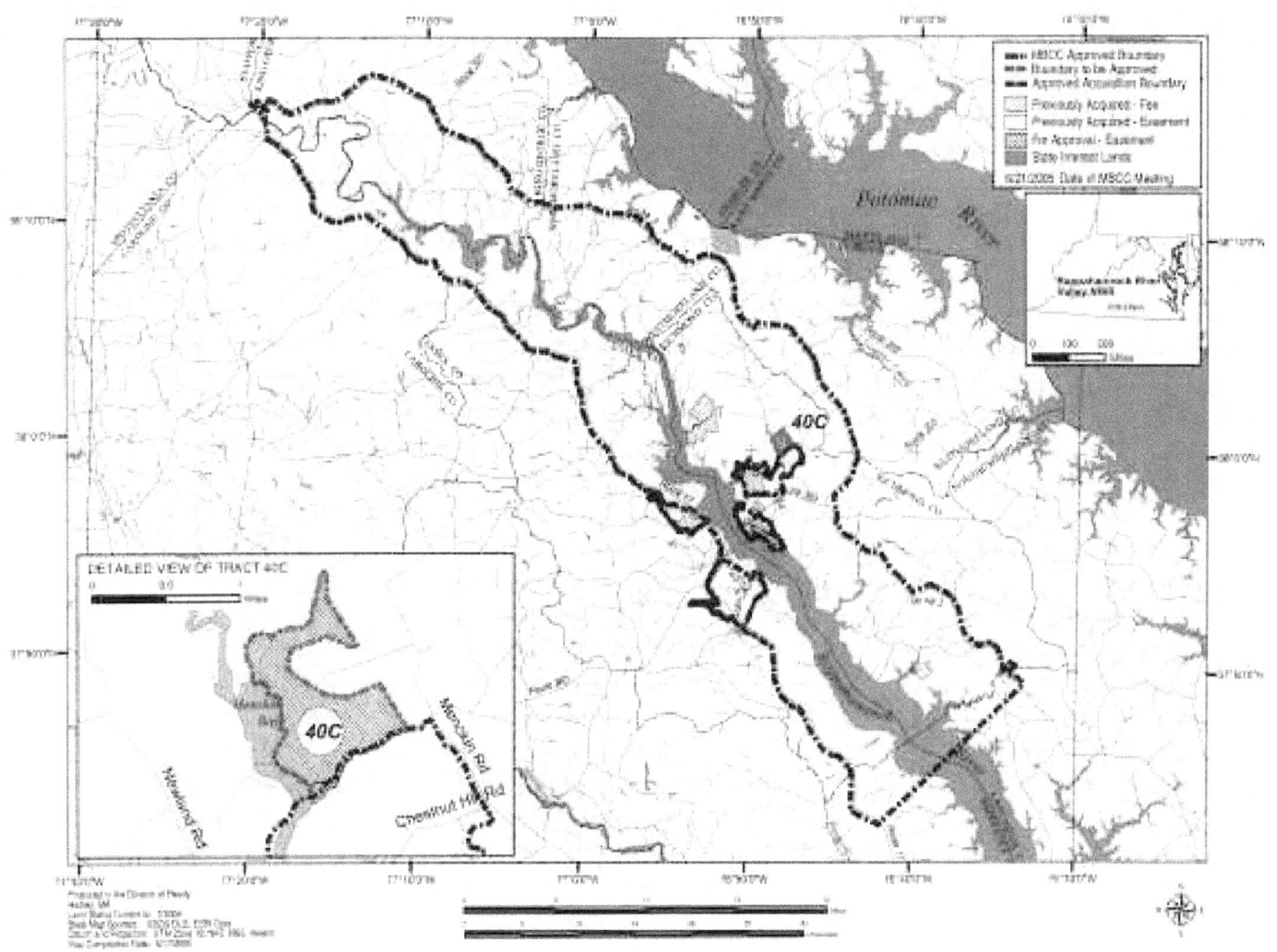

Red River National Wildlife Refuge

Caddo, Bossier, Desota, Red River, and Natchitoches Parishes, Louisiana

Red River National Wildlife Refuge was established on October 13, 2000, under authority of the Red River National Wildlife Refuge Act (Public Law 106300) to preserve, protect and restore 50,000 acres in five refuge units along a 280mile stretch of the Red River in northwest Louisiana. To date, 7,720 acres have been acquired at this refuge with an additional 1,103 acres being leased.

The purposes of Red River NWR are to restore native plants and animal communities in the Red River basin; to provide habitat for migratory waterfowl and other wildlife. The Red River Valley is part of a major continental migration corridor for migratory birds funneling through the mid continent from as far north as the Arctic Circle and as far south as South America. This refuge provides wintering habitat for mallards, pintails, gadwall, wigeon, greenwinged teal, and wood ducks, and contributes to the goals of the North American Waterfowl Management Plan. Restoration of native habitats will benefit resident and migratory waterfowl as well a wide array of other species. In addition, the refuge offers recreational, research, and educational opportunities.

The Commission approved the 23,686 acre refuge boundary addition and price approval for a 1,732 acre tract on September 21, 2005.

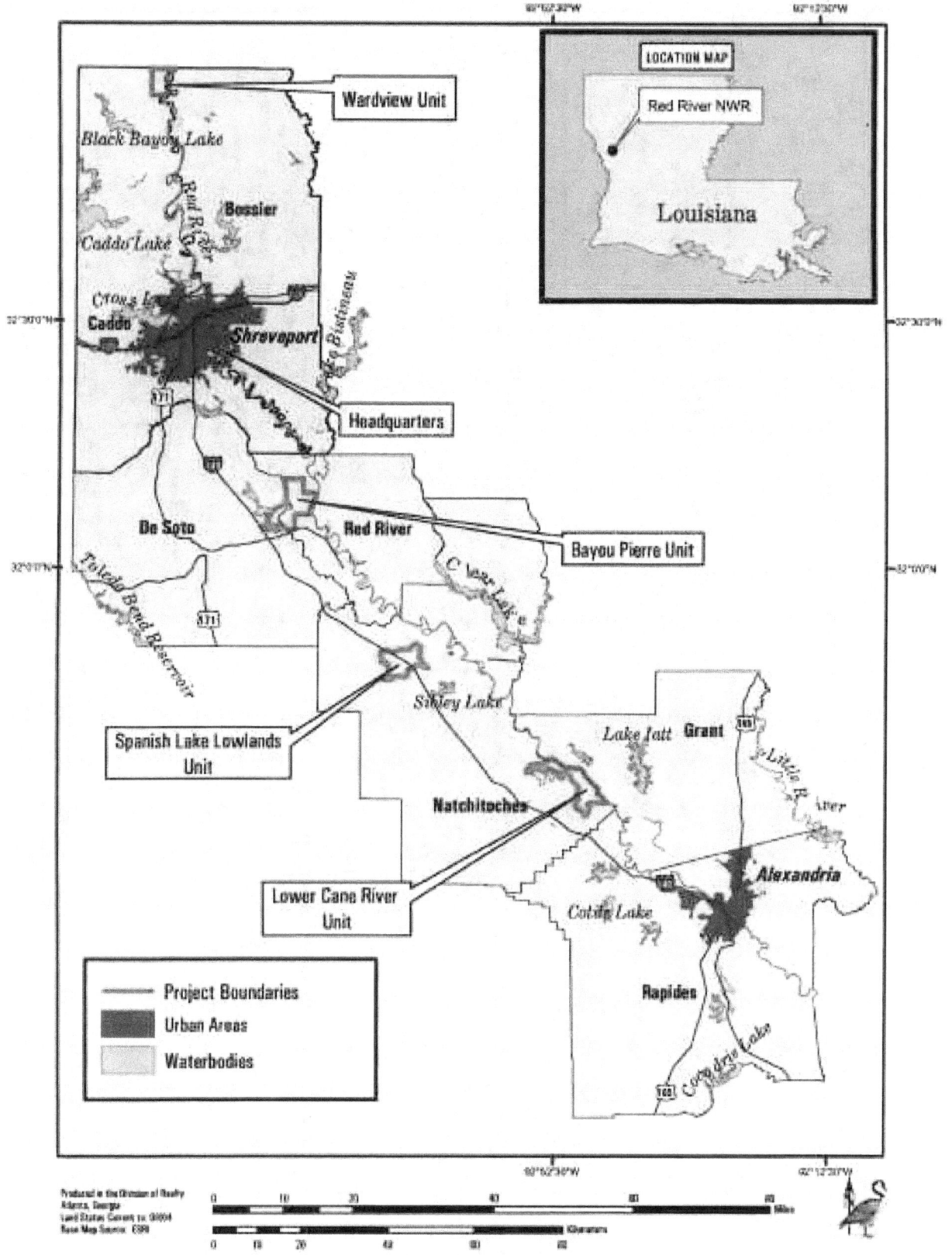

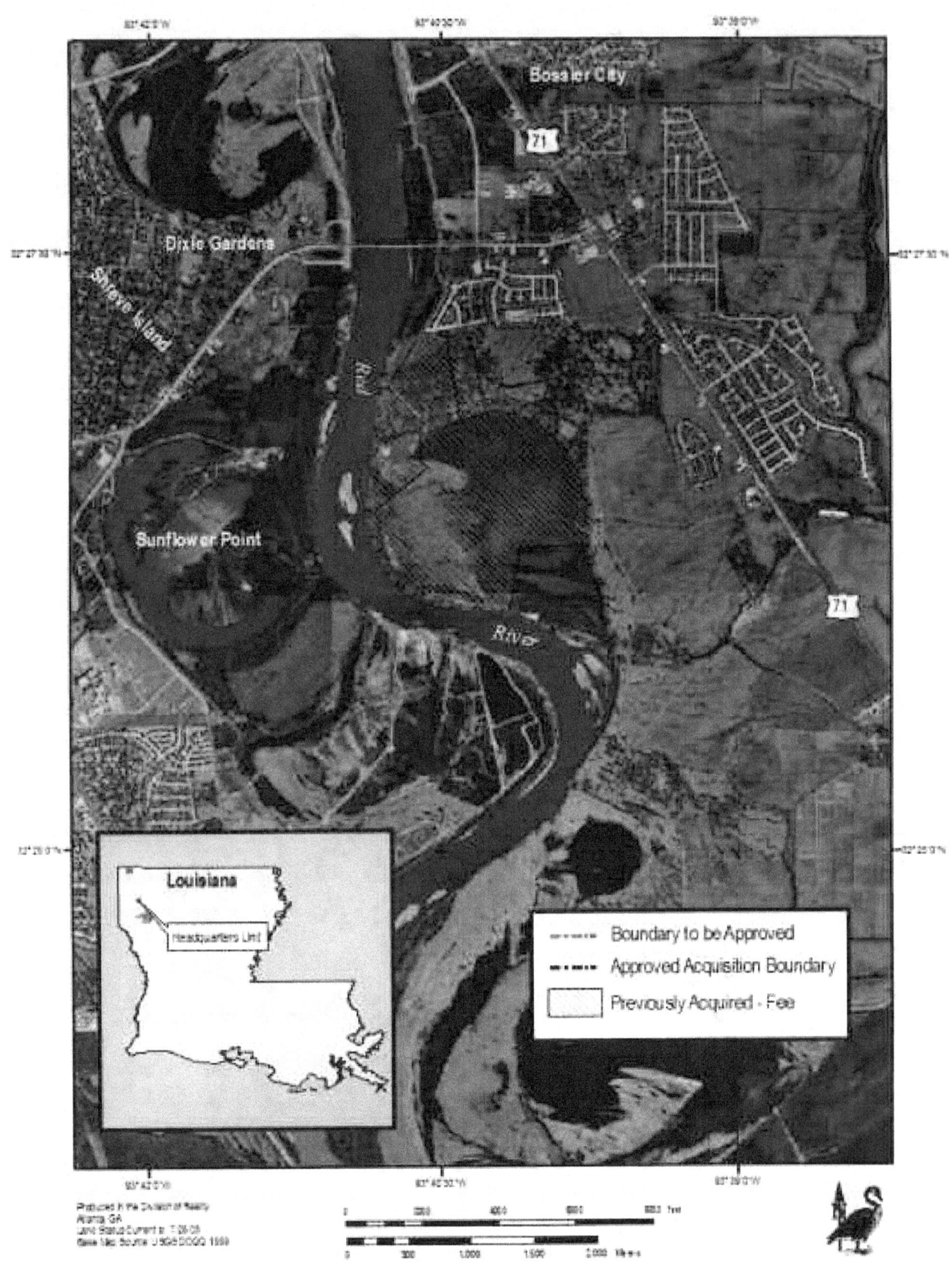

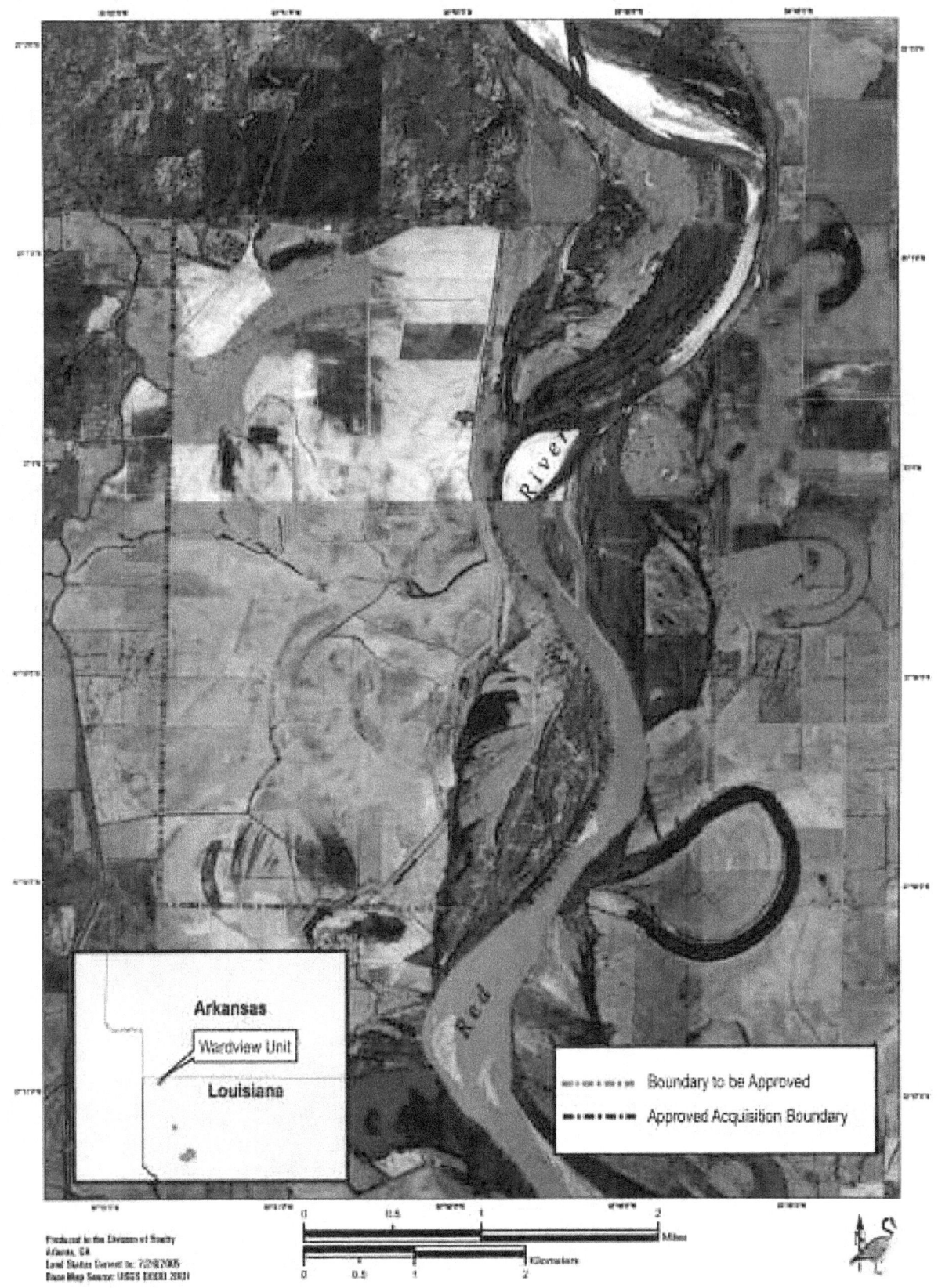

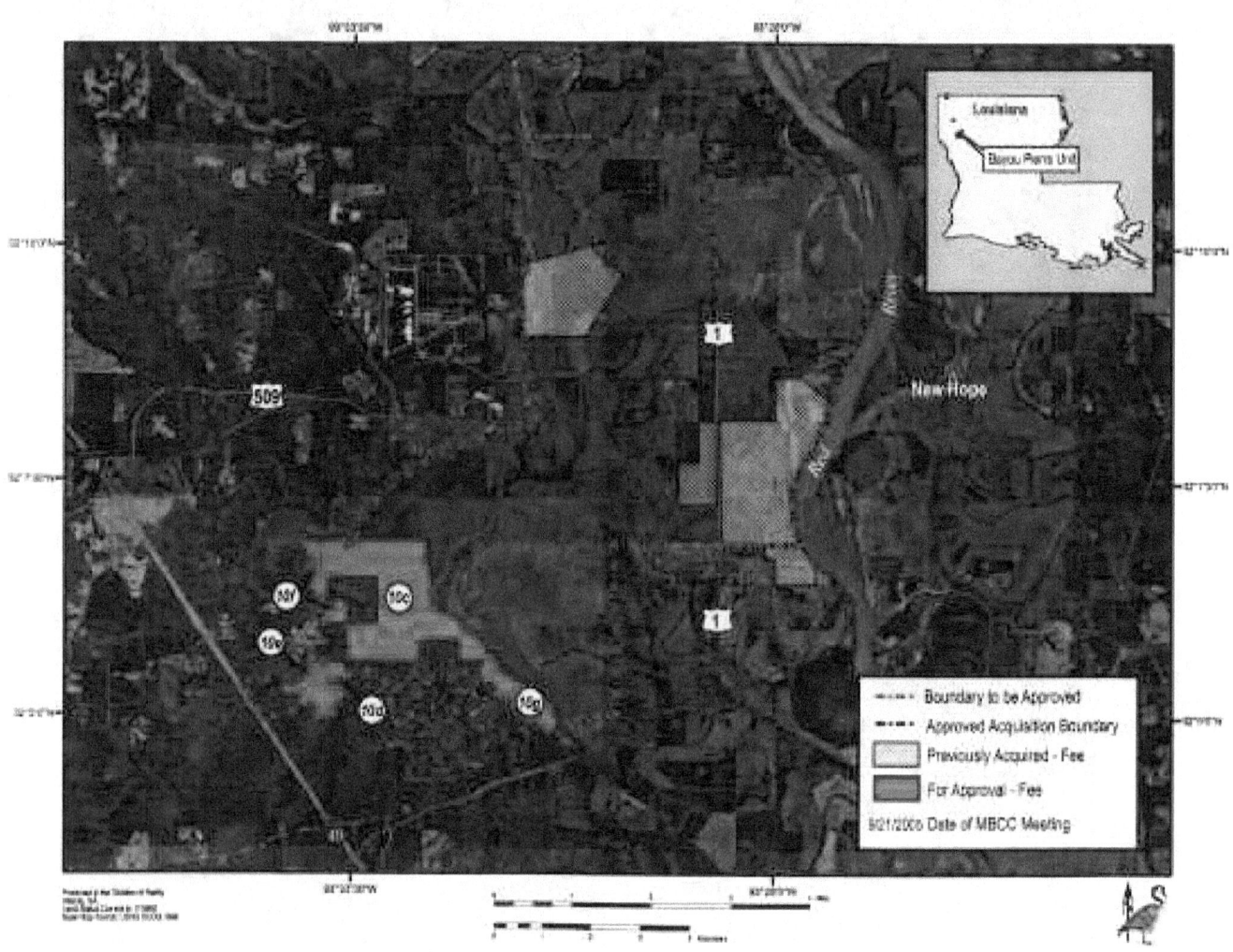

San Bernard National Wildlife Refuge
Brazoria County, Texas

The San Bernard National Wildlife Refuge was approved by the Migratory Bird Conservation Commission on February 27, 1968. To date, 38,513 acres have been acquired. In 1997, the Austin's Woods Conservation Plan authorizing the acquisition of up to 28,000 acres of satellite units to San Bernard was approved. To date, 10,402 acres have been acquired through transfer from the Federal Deposit Insurance Corporation or through donations from various entities, or with funds approved by North American Wetlands Council Act, with funds obtained from mitigation, and by Migratory Bird Conservation Commission approval for the Austin's Woods Unit.

The proposed area is part of a productive and valuable wetland complex providing wintering, migration, and resident habitat for waterfowl, wading birds, neotropical migratory birds, and other wetland-dependent wildlife species. Thousands of waterfowl winter in the area. Mottled ducks, a species of concern, use the area, as well as green-winged teal, gadwalls, and black-bellied whistling ducks. This proposed acquisition is within the Mid-Coast Initiative of the Gulf Coast Joint Venture of the North American Waterfowl Management Plan.

The Commission approved the 197 acre refuge boundary addition and price approval on June 21, 2005. The Commission also approved a 1,031 acre refuge boundary addition and price approval on September 21, 2005.

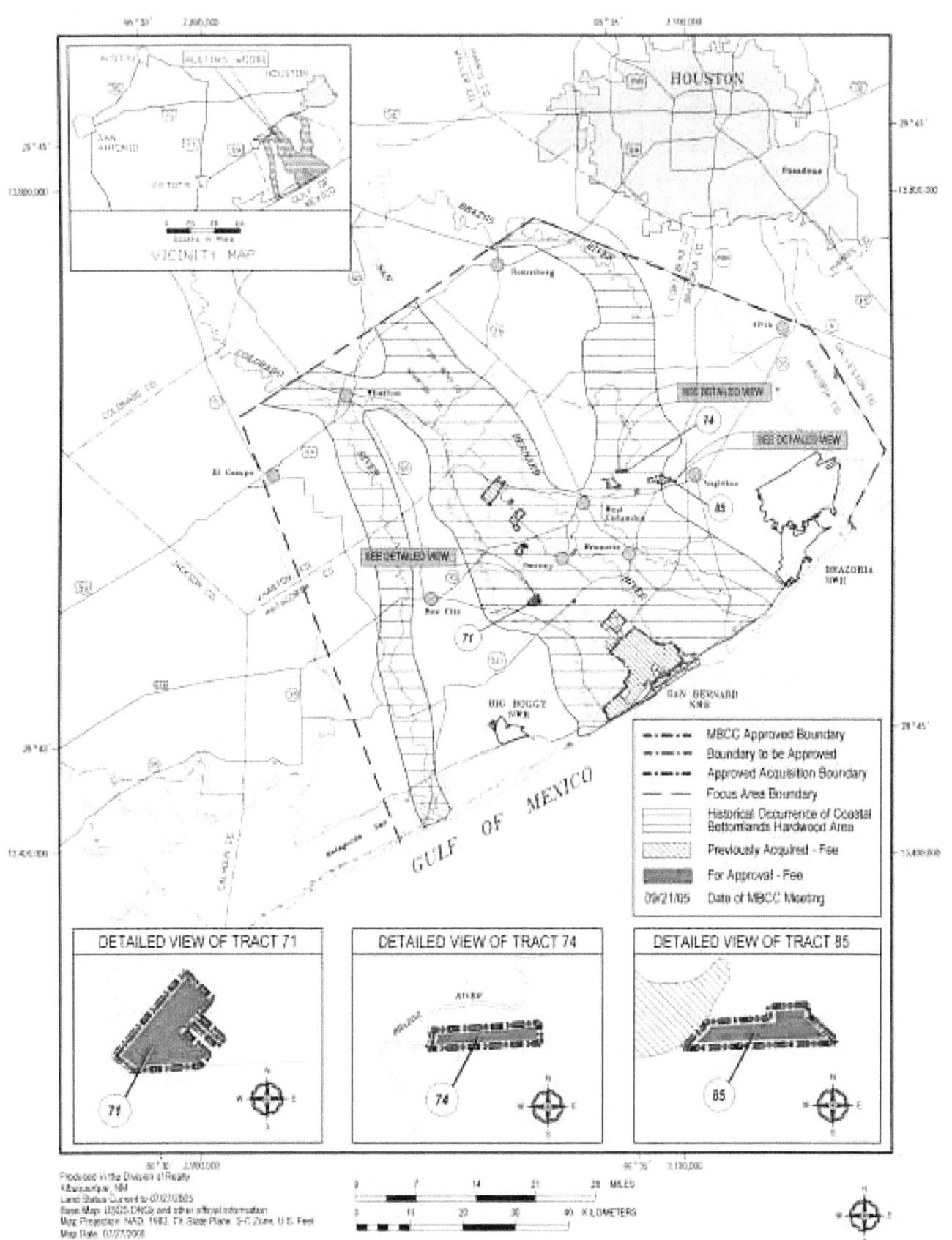

**Silvio O. Conte
National Fish and Wildlife Refuge**
Coos County, New Hampshire

The Silvio O. Conte National Fish and Wildlife Refuge (Refuge) was launched with the introduction of legislation by the late Congressman Silvio O. Conte which authorized a national fish and wildlife refuge within the Connecticut River watershed. Congressman Conte was a member of Congress for over 30 years and served on the Migratory Bird Conservation Commission for about 27 years. After his death, in his honor, Congress renamed the legislation as the Silvio O. Conte National Fish and Wildlife Refuge Act.

The Final Environmental Impact Statement (FEIS) for the Silvio O. Conte Refuge was completed and a Record of Decision authorizing the Refuge was signed by the Regional Director on December 13, 1995. Within the 7.2 million acre Connecticut River watershed, 65 Special Focus Areas important for resource protection were identified in Connecticut, Massachusetts, New Hampshire, and Vermont. The Refuge was officially established on October 3, 1997 with the acquisition of the 3.8 acre Third Island, located in the Connecticut River in Deerfield, Massachusetts. Approximately 31,045 acres of a proposed 91,500 acres have been acquired to date. The Pondicherry Division was established with the purchase of three tracts (670 acres) from one land owner on December 22, 2000.

The area known as Pondicherry is a basin that includes four ponds, the Johnís River, forested and emergent wetlands, bogs, spruce-fir forests, and northern mixed hardwoods. The importance of Pondicherry to a wide variety of migratory birds and other wildlife has been recognized since the late 1800s. In 1972 the area was designated a National Natural Landmark and in 2003, the first Important Bird Area in New Hampshire. The FEIS identified the Pondicherry as one of 65 Special Focus Areas in the Connecticut River watershed for its importance to migratory birds. There have been 233 species of birds documented using the Pondicherry area and 128 species use it for nesting. This northern forest wetland complex specifically provides habitat for 28 species of waterfowl of which eight species nest. Black ducks, wood ducks, mallard, hooded merganser, blue-winged teal, and ring-necked ducks are all commonly seen using Refuge wetlands.

The Commission approved the 825 acre refuge boundary addition and price approval for a 516 acre tract on March 16, 2005.

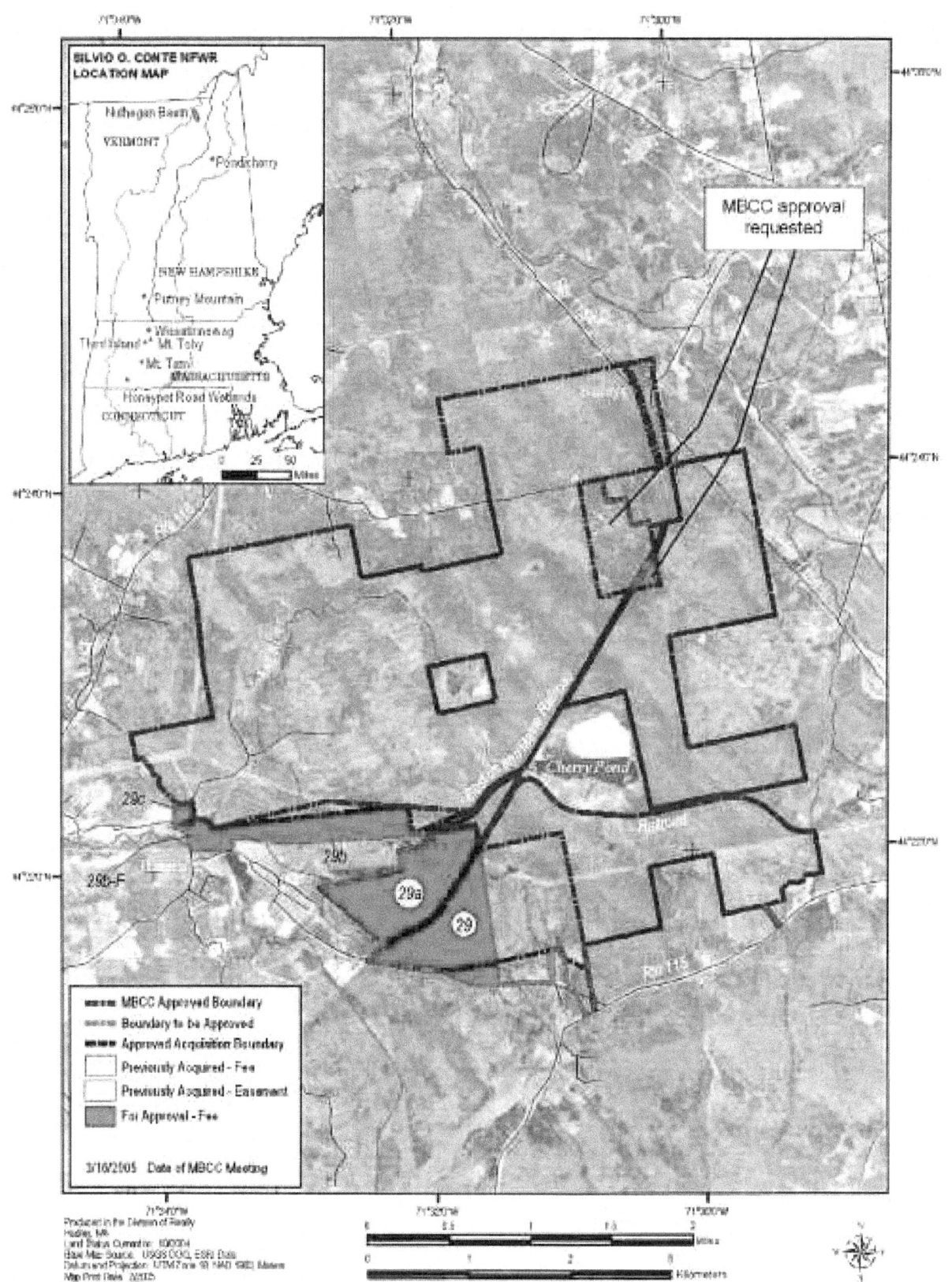

Trinity River National Wildlife Refuge
Liberty County, Texas

The Trinity River National Wildlife
Refuge (Refuge) was established on
January 3, 1994, with the purchase of
4,400 acres of bottomland hardwood and
associated habitats in Liberty County,
Texas. These lands were purchased with
Land and Water Conservation Fund
dollars totaling $3,270,000. Since 1994, an
additional 4,195 acres have been
purchased with LWCF dollars totaling
$1,941,500. On June 14, 1994, the
Migratory Bird Conservation
Commission approved the initial MBCC
boundary for the Refuge, encompassing
19,220 acres. Since 1994, the MBCC
boundary has been expanded by the
Service to include another 10,498 acres.

The Trinity River NWR protects remnant
bottomland hardwood and associated
wetland habitats for migrating, wintering
and breeding waterfowl. Additionally, it
represents one of the few remaining high
quality areas for waterfowl in East Texas.
It provides essential foraging and/or
roosting habitat for the wood duck,
mallard, gadwall, widgeon, green and
blue-winged teal, lesser scaup and
mottled duck. Mature cavity trees
dispersed throughout the area provide
important nesting habitat for wood ducks
and black-bellied whistling ducks.

The Commission approved the 98 acre
refuge boundary addition and price
approval on March 16, 2005. The
Commission also approved a 330 acre
refuge boundary addition and price
approval on June 21, 2005. In addition,
the Commission approved a 3 acre refuge
boundary addition and price approval on
September 21, 2005.

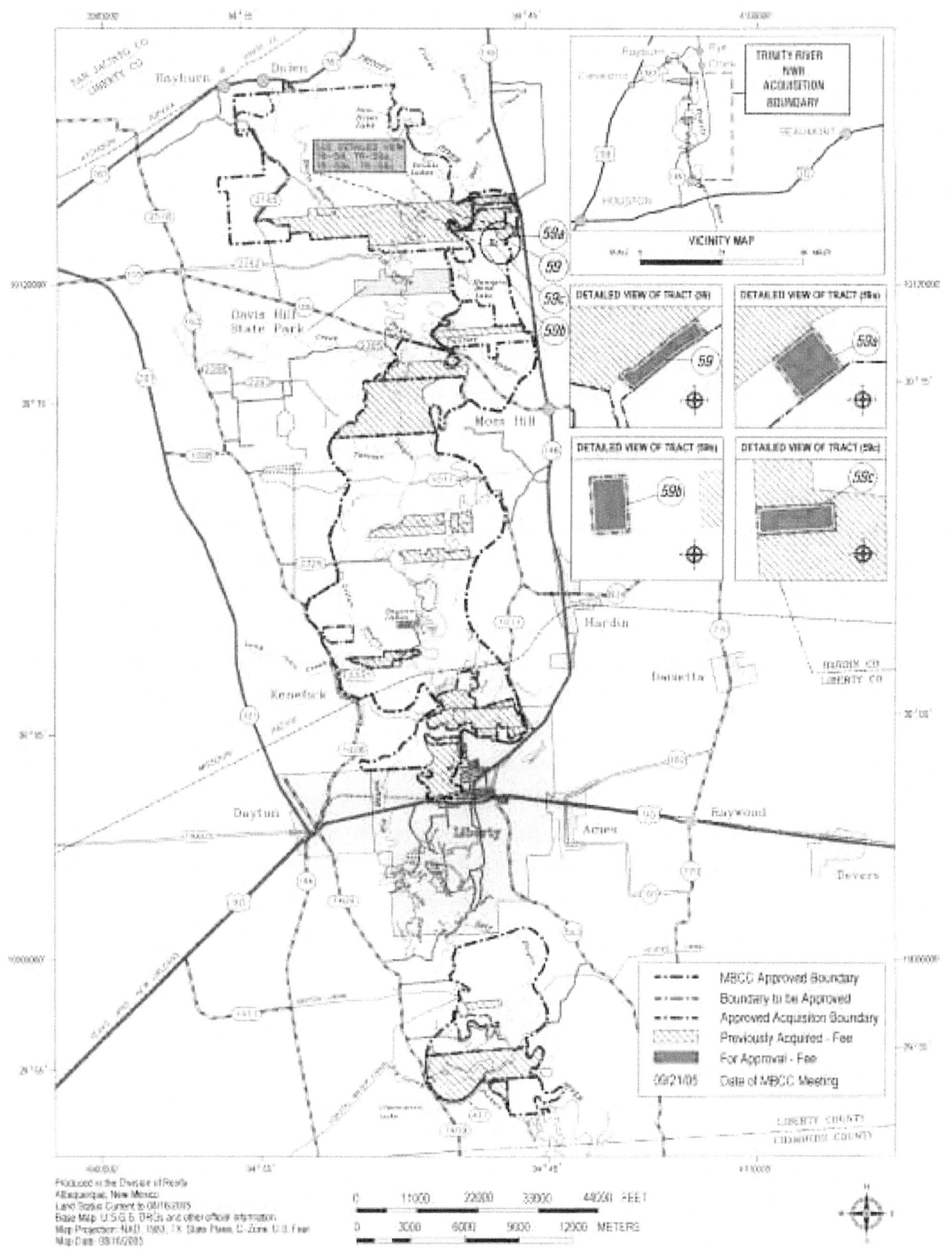

Membership of the National Migratory Bird Conservation Commission

Fiscal Year	Secretary of the Interior[1]	Secretary of Agriculture[2]	Secretary of Commerce[2]	Secretary of Transportation[2]	Administrator of Environmental Protection Agency[2]	Members on Part of the Senate		Members on Part of the House		Secretary to the Commission
						Harry B. Hawes	Peter Norbeck	Sam D. McReynolds	Ernest R. Ackerman	
1929	Roy L. Wilbur	Arthur M. Hyde	Robert P. Lamont			Harry B. Hawes	Peter Norbeck	Sam D. McReynolds	Ernest R. Ackerman	Rudolph Dieffenbach
1930										
1931										
1932									August H. Anderson	
1933	Harold L. Ickes	Henry A. Wallace	Daniel C. Roper			Key Pittman			Roy O. Woodruff	
1934									Chester C. Bolton	
1935										
1936										
1937									James Wolfenden	
1938			Harry L. Hopkins				Charles L. McNary			
1939										
1940			Jessie H. Jones					John J. Cochran		
1941		Claude R. Wickard				George L. Radcliffe				
1942										
1943										
1944							Vacant			
1945		Clinton P. Anderson	Henry A. Wallace			A. Willis Robertson	C. Wayland Brooks		Walter E. Brehm	Arthur A. Riemer
1946	Julius A. Krug		W. Averell Harriman							
1947		Charles F. Brannon	Charles W. Sawyer				Raymond E. Baldwin	Frank M. Karsten		
1948										
1949							Vacant			
1950	Oscar L. Chapman						John W. Bricker			
1951										
1952									August H. Anderson	
1953	Douglas McKay	Ezra Taft Benson	Sinclair Weeks							
1954										
1955										
1956	Fred A. Seaton									
1957						Thomas C. Hennings, Jr.			Leon H. Gavin	Albert J. Rissman
1958			Lewis L. Strauss				Roman L. Hruska			
1959			Frederick H. Mueller			Lee Metcalf				
1960										
1961	Stewart L. Udall	Orville L. Freeman	Luther H. Hodges							
1962										
1963										
1964									George A. Gooding	F.G. Spoden Jr.
1965			John T. Connor						Silvio O. Conte	
1966										
1967			Alexander B. Trowbridge	Alan S. Boyd						
1968								John D. Dingell		
1969	Walter J. Hickel	Clifford M. Hardin		John A. Volpe		Joseph D. Tydings	Henry L. Bellman			
1970										
1971	Roger C.B. Morton	Earl L. Butz				Lee Metcalf				Walter R. McAllester
1972										
1973				Claude S. Brinegar						
1974										
1975	Stanley Hathaway			William T. Coleman		Quentin N. Burdick				
1976	Thomas S. Kleppe									
1977	Cecil D. Andrus	Bob Bergland		Brook Adams		Floyd K. Haskell				
1978										
1979				Neil Golldschmidt		David H. Pryor				
1980										
1981	James G. Watt	James R. Block		Drew Lewis			Thad Cochran			
1982										
1983	William P. Clark			Elizabeth H. Dole						
1984										
1985	Donald Hodel									
1986		Richard Lyng								William F. Hartwig
1987				James Burnley IV						
1988										
1989	Manuel Lujan Jr.	Clayton Yeutter		Samuel K. Skinner						
1990					William K. Reilly					
1991		Edward R. Madigan								
1992									Richard T. Schulze	Geoffrey L. Haskett
1993	Bruce Babbitt	Mike Espy			Carol M. Browner				Curt Weldon	
1994		Daniel R. Glickman								
1995										Jeffrey M. Donahoe
1996						John B. Breaux				
1997										
1998										
1999										
2000										
2001	Gale Norton	Ann M. Veneman			Christine Todd-Whitman					
2002						Blanche L. Lincoln				A. Eric Alvarez
2003					Michael O. Leavitt					
2004										
2005		Mike Johanns			Stephen L. Johnson					

Footnotes: 1 - Chairman, 1940 to date; 2 - Chairman, 1929 to 1939; 3 - Member, 1929 to March 1, 1968; 4 - Member, March 2, 1968 to December 12, 1989; 5 - member, December 13, 1989 to date

Migratory Bird Conservation Commission
National Migratory Bird Refuge Areas

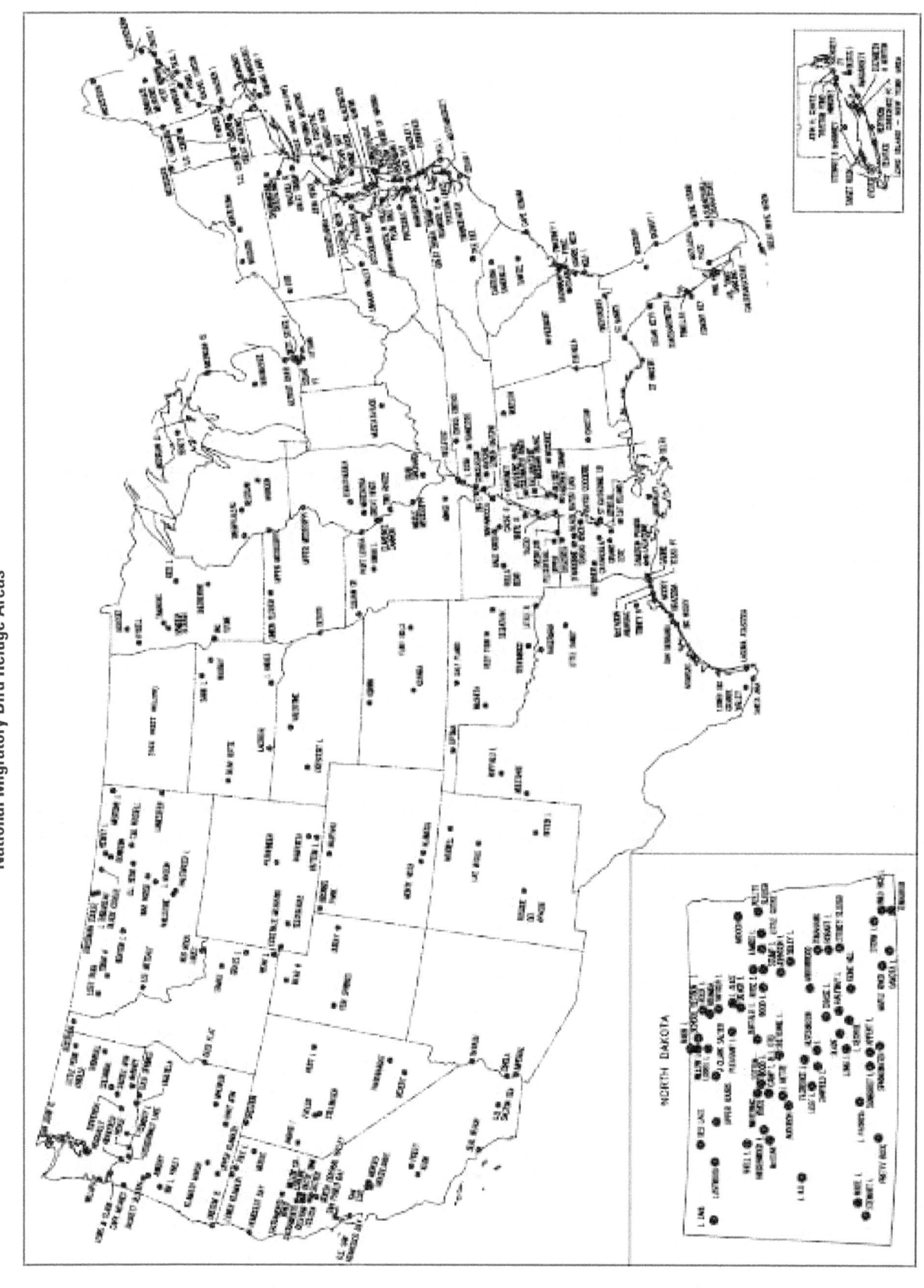

COMPILED IN THE DIVISION OF REALTY

WASHINGTON, DC   SEPTEMBER 30, 2015

Wetland Management Districts of the National Wildlife Refuge System

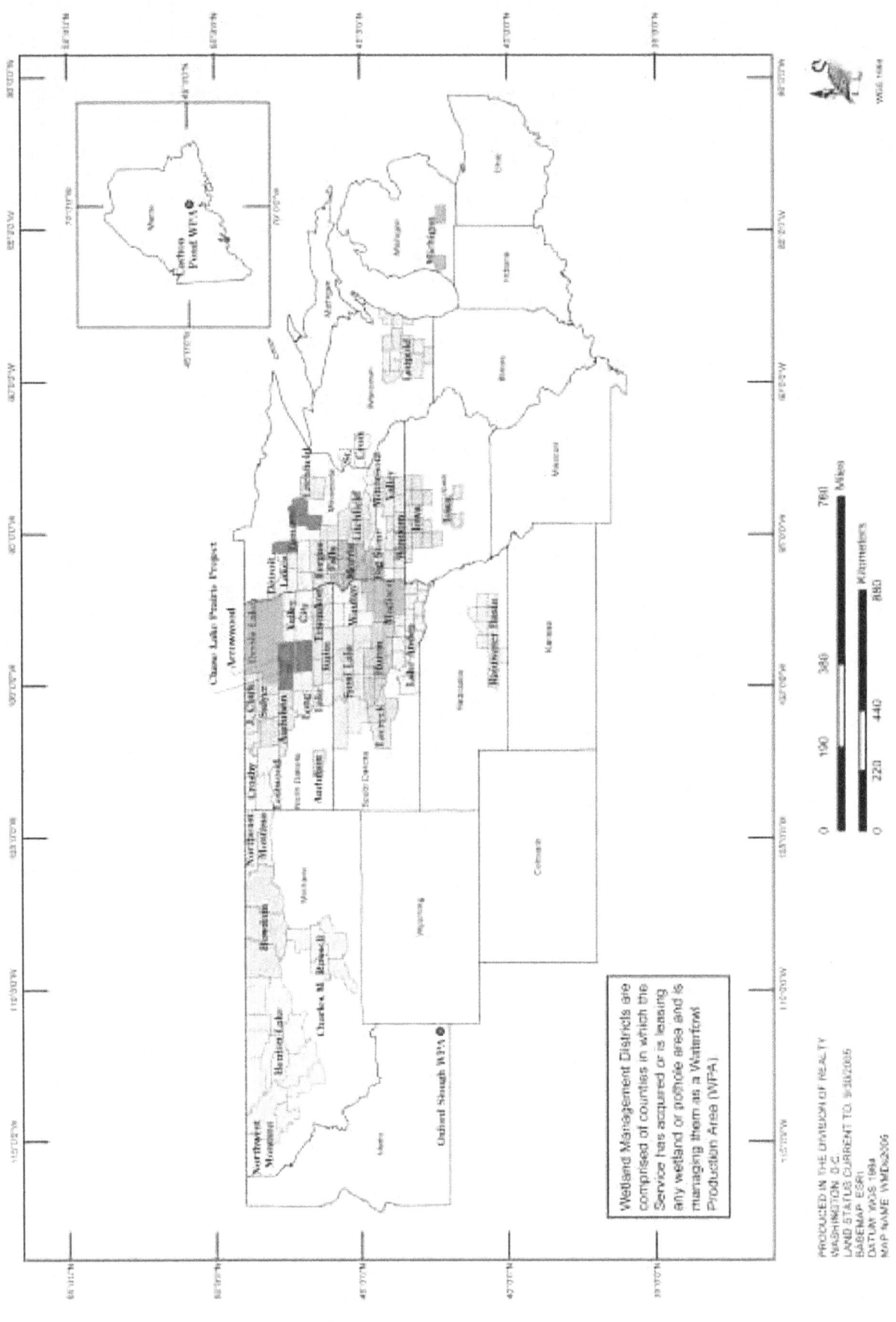

Notes on Tables One and Two

The information contained in this report includes those acquisitions and dispositions of land and interests therein that are purchased with Migratory Bird Conservation Fund monies or acquired under the authority of the Migratory Bird Conservation Act. It also includes other migratory bird areas such as those that are transferred to the Fish and Wildlife Service under the authority of Public Law 80-537 to carry out a migratory bird management program (these will appear on Table 1).

In an ongoing effort to improve data quality, the figures in Tables One and Two may show minor changes from previous annual reports. Lands in which the Service previously acquired a less-than-fee interest (leases and easements) may be purchased in fee during the year, and the number of easement or lease acres will show a decrease and the number of purchased acres an increase. The acreage appearing in the Approvals and Summary of Land Acquisitions sections of this report will not appear in Tables One or Two until after the tracts are acquired and the funds are actually expended. Also, a newly approved refuge will not appear on Table One until the tracts are acquired.

For information on all lands and interests under U.S. Fish and Wildlife Service control, refer to the *Annual Report of Lands Under Control of the U.S. Fish and Wildlife Service*. This report can be obtained from the U.S. Fish and Wildlife Service Division of Realty at http://realty.fws.gov or by calling (703) 358-1713.

7,953.19

34,430.66

30,279.82

14,809.95

62,929.57

3,458.67

13,042.89

158,414.72

4,246.52

5,796.54

80.00

7,235.34

7,958.19

44,294.55

7,021.23

6,970.16

10,816.22

22,893.41

910.71

2,590.16

5,566.50

23,269.52

338.64

911.44

2.60

143,953.77

891.15

328.30

117,683.13

6,406.79

538.25

3,724.48

394.35

12,489.93

4,940.33

391,401.99

14,163.48

5,125.82

10,578.34

1,110.60

2,774.29

43,909.42

7,110.63

2,482.53

8,033.20

7,802.22

22,623.38

18,463.36

10,778.00

2,039.64

24,548.03

24,909.61

48,799.10

6,077.00

17,561.46

8,823.99

69,342.15

4,699.95

11.94

5,642.73

5,859.64

5,335.58

25,685.51

2,286.27

4,423.43

3.79

3,849.81

24.00

1,677.02

215.73

1,966.46

597.39

9,362.75

11,585.42

3,209.85

2,070.00

35,191.38

9,166.80

19,051.39

7,373.11

35,271.85

2,794.14

3,749.98

2,107.93

21,661.05

11,492.97

12,459.44

15,551.97

2,728.00

920.00

1,360.92

3,868.48

2,792.52

31,533.71

1,568.81

3,392.87

4,324.20

73,098.09

1,615,321.39

5,382.74

572,876.15

13,154.27

11,137.27

7,651.45

4,746.05

57,191.10

3,698.59

60.40

2,714.10

8,562.62

209.23

80.09

2,571.58

8,313.64

26,109.70

50,180.18

8,438.94

21,062.43

907.75

15,942.86

640.00

1,563.72

313.23

1,013.47

19,547.14

6,591.40

568.35

478.90

2,007.91

12,095.54

4,033.12

320.00

3,823.19

288.41

1,915.29

26,903.99

760.00

800.00

5,505.96

297.30

797.30

3,347.64

1,550.18

2,230.40

685.90

327.51

440.00

1,040.00

2,620.38

280.00

6,551.24

8,922.34

4,332.81

20,800.00

8,075.37

2,492.33

3,116.83

607.05

40,884.98

6,618.13

1,079.61

8,907.37

5,673.11

993.17

428.52

241.90

66,287.18

1,430.04

12,483.28

100.00

151.20

5,639.43

4,740.22

8,861.49

11,556.10

11,828.30

51,359.46

114,412.08

44,413.88

1,878.13

86,817.92

58,861.43

5,809.10

2,087.50

18,699.89

17,992.24

12,138.24

6,560.48

8,994.70

1,123.27

133.70

874.40

422.99

3,501.68

7,723.48

29,596.27

965.92

15,505.39

329.38

161,485.93

1,046.02

16,532.07

16,160.80

8.37

21,405.32

6,198.83

9,259.32

1,968.34

27,230.22

(41) "   " MASSACHUSETTS AND NEW HAMPSHIRE
(42) "   " VERMONT AND NEW HAMPSHIRE

*   - COUNTED IN ANOTHER STATE
**   - DENOTES INTERESTS TRANSFERRED BY THE FSA
FSA - FARM SERVICE AGENCY (FORMERLY FARMERS HOME ADMINISTRATION, DEPARTMENT OF AGRICULTURE)

391.33

2,725.95

5,401.16

669.05

809.70

41.00

494.16

549.42

1,509.84

1,068.21

77.08

15,015.28

1,313.62

43.00

14,029.89

3,289.31

15,801.48

1,908.86

4,552.65

5,862.59

2,094.83

10,872.06

2,022.12

2,179.05

1,120.00

14,716.61

1,453.03

11.00

1,159.13

630.11

9,587.59

5,549.16

225.07

3,229.07

8,767.46

2,637.13

5,218.23

920.27

7,447.05

428.00

40.00

9,127.01

7,581.62

1,828.48

16,776.85

486.42

6,364.58

1,783.32

649.47

3,049.93

140.78

471.14

26,888.68

32,457.32

58,525.78

24,762.83

46,236.04

15,415.89

8,049.31

1,202.60

20,322.55

57,826.46

43,577.58

41,863.84

54,426.11

28,124.50

13,052.17

25,298.25

7,653.55

32,795.33

10,882.82

24,366.23

39,153.60

1,426.90

55,907.22

2,260.13

12,893.39

99.50

1,105.90

52,755.86

956.80

129,279.15

25,109.41

9,720.03

3,888.86

2,019.01

25,188.51

32,468.73

477.72

10,514.83

26,968.61

5,568.69

56,771.57

29,473.97

4,075.99

1,329.99

21,262.32

344.00

1,591.08

621.98

249.79

259.97

1,045.07

709.91

232.30

47

North American Wetlands Conservation Fund (Summary) Fiscal Year 2005

The Migratory Bird Conservation Commission approved 84 standard wetland conservation project proposals for funding in Fiscal Year 2005 under the North American Wetlands Conservation Act. A total of $60,526,249 from the North American Wetlands Conservation Fund (Fund), together with $271,317,853 in partner funds, are supporting 42 projects in the United States, 27 in Canada, and 15 in Mexico. The following tables provide summary and detailed allocation information.

Fiscal Year 2005
Projects Approved by the Migratory Bird Conservation Commission and Active Under the North American Wetlands Conservation Act

Country	Number of Projects	Act Funds	Partner Funds	Acres Affected
U.S.	42	$37,163,758	$237,120,536	1,256,295
Canada	27	$20,977,334	$30,566,171	427,934
Mexico	15	$2,385,157	$3,631,146	251,206
Total	84	$60,526,249	$271,317,853	1,935,435

Additionally, 38 small grants were approved, totaling $1,620,088 from the Fund, supported by $7,927,543 in partner funds and affecting 14,464 acres.

United States Wetlands Conservation Standard Grant Proposals Approved by the Migratory Bird Conservation Commission For Fiscal Year 2005

Table Three

Project Name	State	NAWCA Grant ($)	Non-Fed Match	Non-Fed Non-Match	Federal Non-Match	Total Partners	Total Cost	Total Acres	MBCC Approval
Bonneau Ferry	SC	1,000,000.00	5,205,000.00	6,365,307.00	33,269,747.00	44,840,054.00	45,840,054.00	11,775.00	9/8/2004
Buzzards Bay Watershed: Chapin White	MA	1,000,000.00	2,024,700.00	20,000.00	0.00	2,044,700.00	3,044,700.00	320.50	3/16/2005
Buzzards Bay Watershed: Nasketucket Bay Field & Marsh	MA	285,000.00	1,156,853.00	0.00	0.00	1,156,853.00	1,441,853.00	112.60	3/16/2005
Buzzards Bay Watershed: Nasketucket Bay Vivieros	MA	1,000,000.00	3,098,000.00	20,000.00	0.00	3,118,000.00	4,118,000.00	252.00	3/16/2005
Catahoula NWR Restoration & Expansion, I	LA	1,000,000.00	2,228,108.00	0.00	0.00	2,228,108.00	3,228,108.00	18,372.00	9/8/2004
Chase Lake Area Wetland, Project VI	ND	1,000,000.00	1,517,293.00	0.00	128,475.00	1,645,768.00	2,645,768.00	62,271.00	9/8/2004
Chenier Plain Coastal Wetlands Conservation, II	LA,TX	998,952.00	6,256,930.00	0.00	645,290.00	6,902,220.00	7,901,172.00	10,719.00	9/8/2004
Clayhole Swamp	GA	1,000,000.00	2,826,704.00	2,222,500.00	1,000,000.00	6,049,204.00	7,049,204.00	7,336.00	3/16/2005
Conservation of Priority Wetland Bird Focus Areas, Teton River Basin	ID,WY	1,000,000.00	13,671,151.00	0.00	334,301.00	14,005,452.00	15,005,452.00	2,040.00	6/21/2005
Downeast Lakes Forestry Partnership	ME	1,000,000.00	5,570,000.00	18,400,000.00	0.00	23,970,000.00	24,970,000.00	339,080.00	9/8/2004
Grand Kankakee Habitat Restoration, Project IV	IN	1,000,000.00	3,061,020.00	49,560.00	874,703.00	3,985,283.00	4,985,283.00	1,596.00	9/8/2004
Greater Pleasant Bay Project Area	ME	650,000.00	1,310,500.00	8,000.00	10,000.00	1,328,500.00	1,978,500.00	762.00	9/8/2004
Hanson Marsh Hydrologic Restoration	LA	765,728.00	2,134,000.00	19,428.50	6,200.00	2,159,628.50	2,925,356.50	45,366.00	9/8/2004
Izembek NWR Complex, Phase III	AK	750,000.00	1,545,625.00	0.00	0.00	1,545,625.00	2,295,625.00	18,045.00	9/8/2004
Lake County Closed Basin Project	OR	1,000,000.00	1,169,393.00	90,000.00	483,775.00	1,743,168.00	2,743,168.00	5,230.00	9/8/2004
LMV Priority Sites, Louisiana, Phase I	LA	987,753.00	1,765,790.00	1,662,500.00	6,048.00	3,434,338.00	4,422,091.00	8,799.00	9/8/2004
Maine Forest Ecosystem Project (MFEP)	ME	1,000,000.00	3,000,000.00	26,429,265.00	0.00	29,429,265.00	30,429,265.00	476,291.00	9/8/2004
Manchac Wildlife Management Area Prairie Shoreline Protection	LA	1,000,000.00	2,293,595.00	0.00	0.00	2,293,595.00	3,293,595.00	8,325.00	9/8/2004
Maurepas/Pontchartrain Habitat Conservation Effort I	LA	1,000,000.00	2,300,000.00	800,000.00	0.00	3,100,000.00	4,100,000.00	69,500.00	9/8/2004
McPherson Valley Wetlands, V	KS	646,500.00	1,321,378.00	22,727.00	0.00	1,344,105.00	1,990,605.00	325.00	9/8/2004
Middle Mississippi River Ecosystems Project	IL	704,500.00	1,422,683.00	0.00	15,000.00	1,437,683.00	2,142,183.00	3,369.00	3/16/2005
Middle Rio Grande Wetlands, Project II	NM	1,000,000.00	2,596,130.00	0.00	822,673.00	3,418,803.00	4,418,803.00	2,415.00	3/16/2005
Minnesota Marshes, I	MN	1,000,000.00	2,022,649.00	0.00	17,433.00	2,040,082.00	3,040,082.00	4,530.00	9/8/2004
Missouri/Yellowstone River Confluence Land Acquisition, I	ND	774,748.00	784,924.00	114,116.00	1,253,300.00	$2,152,340.00	2,927,088.00	1,523.00	9/8/2004
North Carolina Riparian Corridors, I	NC	1,000,000.00	6,947,835.00	120,000.00	0.00	7,067,835.00	8,067,835.00	4,502.00	3/16/05
North Dakota Great Plains, Project IV	ND	225,000.00	455,950.50	0.00	93,200.00	549,150.50	774,150.50	4,077.70	3/16/2005
Northern Accomack Habitat Conservation Initiative	VA	1,000,000.00	3,318,758.00	2,017,500.00	0.00	5,336,258.00	6,336,258.00	4,650.00	3/16/2005
Prairie Wetland Heritage Conservation Initiative, III	MN	1,000,000.00	1,965,283.00	80,292.00	2,428,224.00	4,473,799.00	5,473,799.00	9,330.60	9/8/2004
San Juan Islands, I	WA	1,000,000.00	2,215,120.00	27,000.00	0.00	2,242,120.00	3,242,120.00	668.00	6/21/2005
San Pablo Bay Tidal Wetlands Habitat Restoration, Project II	CA	999,790.00	12,602,345.00	0.00	0.00	12,602,345.00	13,602,135.00	2,434.00	6/21/2005
South Dakota Threatened Habitats, II	SD	$826,000.00	1,304,020.00	0.00	8,400,000.00	9,704,020.00	10,530,020.00	77,705.00	3/16/2005
Southeast Wisconsin Coastal Habitat Initiative, IV	WI	998,400.00	2,043,500.00	0.00	0.00	2,043,500.00	3,041,900.00	2,041.00	9/8/2004
Southern Tip Ecological Partnership, I	VA	918,736.00	2,402,000.00	0.00	76,900.00	2,478,900.00	3,397,636.00	2,550.00	3/16/2005
Southwest Indiana Habitat Expansion Project	IN	1,000,000.00	2,666,920.00	3,200,000.00	620,000.00	6,486,920.00	7,486,920.00	9,139.00	3/16/2005
St. Marys River Bird Migration Corridor, II	MI	1,000,000.00	4,711,000.00	0.00	0.00	4,711,000.00	5,711,000.00	1,418.00	9/8/2004
Suisun Marsh Managed Wetlands Enhancement Project	CA	1,000,000.00	2,199,634.00	0.00	0.00	2,199,634.00	3,199,634.00	24,665.00	9/8/2004
West Bay Conservation Corridor Wetlands Restoration & Acquisition	TX	1,000,000.00	1,008,000.00	0.00	0.00	1,008,000.00	2,008,000.00	1,560.00	3/16/2005
Wetlands Restoration Within the West Gulf Coastal Plain, II	TX	671,583.00	1,288,679.00	55,000.00	484,560.00	1,828,239.00	2,499,822.00	3,939.00	3/16/2005
White Oak River/Quaternary Tract	NC	481,842.00	1,053,258.00	100,000.00	25,000.00	1,178,258.00	1,660,100.00	1,443.20	3/16/2005
Winnebago system - Rush Lake Initiative	WI	1,000,000.00	2,531,928.00	0.00	57,888.00	2,589,816.00	3,589,816.00	6,064.62	9/8/2004
Yolo Basin Wetland Habitat Project, II	CA	1,000,000.00	2,089,500.00	25,000.00	25,000.00	2,139,500.00	3,139,500.00	1,449.00	3/16/2005
Yuma East Wetlands Restoration Project	AZ	479,226.00	958,452.00	535,015.00	1,615,000.00	3,108,467.00	3,587,693.00	304.40	6/21/2005
Number of Projects: 42		37,163,758.00	122,044,608.50	62,383,210.50	52,692,717.00	237,120,536.00	274,284,294.00	1,256,294.62	

United States Wetlands Conservation
Small Grant Proposals
Approved by the Migratory Bird Conservation Commission
For Fiscal Year 2005

Table Three

Project Name	State	NAWCA Grant ($)	Non-Fed Match	Non-Fed Non-Match	Federal Non-Match	Total Partners	Total Cost	Total Acres	MBCC Approval
Ambassador Duck Club Wetland Restoration in Treated Phragmites Area	UT	27,400.00	43,353.00	0.00	0.00	43,353.00	70,753.00	400.00	6/9/2004
Baldwin Flooding Wetland & Grassland Complex	MI	35,000.00	37,180.00	8,000.00	0.00	45,180.00	80,180.00	77.00	6/9/2004
Burleson Wetlands Village Slough & West Roost Renovation	TX	45,000.00	55,000.00	0.00	0.00	55,000.00	100,000.00	140.00	6/9/2004
Camp 19 / Old Railroad Grade Waterfowl Mgmt. Area	WI	19,000.00	19,000.00	0.00	0.00	19,000.00	38,000.00	70.00	6/9/2004
Carpinteria Creek Arundo Removal Project	CA	36,600.00	89,000.00	$0.00	0.00	89,000.00	125,600.00	2.50	6/9/2004
Clinton Lake SRA Trenkel Slough, Unit #2	IL	49,200.00	144,300.00	0.00	0.00	144,300.00	193,500.00	60.00	6/9/2004
Dougherty County Greenspace Acquisition Program - Lower Flint River Basin	GA	50,000.00	88,497.44	0.00	0.00	88,497.44	138,497.44	103.13	6/9/2004
Errol Creek Wetlands & Stream Habitat	OR	50,000.00	663,824.00	0.00	0.00	663,824.00	713,824.00	17.89	6/9/2004
Goose Pond Wildlife Refuge Restoration & Acquisition	MA	36,450.00	87,200.00	0.00	$0.00	87,200.00	123,650.00	100.00	6/9/2004
Headwater Wetlands of Crosswicks Creek	NJ	50,000.00	405,000.00	372,500.00	0.00	777,500.00	827,500.00	50.60	6/9/2004
Iowa Prairie Pothole Upland Habitat Development Project	IA	50,000.00	105,390.00	0.00	0.00	105,390.00	155,390.00	1,038.00	6/9/2004
Joseph Creek Watershed Preservation Project	WA	50,000.00	2,695,000.00	0.00	10,000.00	2,705,000.00	2,755,000.00	10.00	6/9/2004
Lunch Creek Project	AK	50,000.00	170,000.00	0.00	0.00	170,000.00	220,000.00	207.00	6/9/2004
McNamara Ranch Acquisition & Habitat Enhancement	CA	50,000.00	632,000.00	0.00	0.00	632,000.00	682,000.00	108.00	6/9/2004
Middle Mississippi River Ecosystem Project: Rockwood Island	IL	50,000.00	171,000.00	20,500.00	5,000.00	196,500.00	246,500.00	269.47	6/9/2004
Millers Pasture Wetland Project	GA	50,000.00	135,414.79	0.00	0.00	135,414.79	185,414.79	90.00	6/9/2004
North Bay Grays Harbor Coastal Preservation Project	WA	50,000.00	89,000.00	0.00	0.00	89,000.00	139,000.00	60.00	6/9/2004
North Branch Tidal Wetland Acquisition	ME	50,000.00	350,000.00	0.00	0.00	350,000.00	400,000.00	61.00	6/9/2004
Northeastern Indiana Wetland/ Grassland Restoration Program	IN	50,000.00	50,003.00	0.00	30,000.00	80,003.00	130,003.00	110.80	6/920/04
Prairie & Wetland Focus Area - Playa Restoration Project	CO	50,000.00	125,426.00	0.00	14,000.00	139,426.00	189,426.00	200.00	6/9/2004
Project Greenshores Habitat Restoration, Site 2	FL	50,000.00	55,000.00	0.00	0.00	55,000.00	105,000.00	30.00	6/9/2004
Rabbit River Restoration	MN	50,000.00	50,945.45	0.00	8,000.00	58,945.45	108,945.45	415.00	6/9/2004
Raven Run Nature Sanctuary Seasonal Wetland Establishment	KY	6,839.00	6,900.00	0.00	0.00	6,900.00	13,739.00	2.10	6/9/2004
Restoration of Wetlands, La Selva Verde Tract of Laguna Atascosa NWR	TX	21,000.00	21,000.00	0.00	0.00	21,000.00	42,000.00	271.00	6/9/2004
Rio Grande Wetland Protection Project - Higel Ranch	CO	50,000.00	224,210.00	0.00	0.00	224,210.00	274,210.00	200.00	6/9/2004
San Joaquin Basin Wetland Restoration	CA	50,000.00	95,256.00	0.00	0.00	95,256.00	145,256.00	340.00	6/9/2004
Schoodic Bog Acquisition	ME	50,000.00	258,500.00	0.00	0.00	258,500.00	308,500.00	500.00	6/9/2004
Shonhatsi Meadow Wetlands Enhancement	NY	22,213.00	22,213.00	0.00	0.00	22,213.00	44,426.00	7.00	6/9/2004
Spring Creek Enhancement Project	NC	50,000.00	73,200.00	0.00	0.00	73,200.00	123,200.00	80.00	6/9/2004
Sunoco Wetlands Restoration	NJ	22,000.00	32,500.00	0.00	0.00	32,500.00	54,500.00	43.00	6/9/2004
Supplemental Water for the Myrtle Forester - Whitmire Preserve	TX	45,509.20	97,068.64	7,600.00	0.00	104,668.64	150,177.84	900.00	6/9/2004
Three Rivers Wetland Hydrology Enhancement	CA	50,000.00	102,029.00	0.00	0.00	102,029.00	152,029.00	249.00	6/9/2004
Truman Lake Wetland Restoration Partnership	MO	50,000.00	256,000.00	0.00	0.00	256,000.00	306,000.00	770.00	6/9/2004
Union River Estuary Acquisition	WA	43,642.00	87,283.00	0.00	43,642.00	130,925.00	174,567.00	11.39	6/9/2004
Upper Berrys Brook Headwaters Conservation Initiative, Maxam Parcels	NH	41,500.00	203,300.00	0.00	0.00	203,300.00	244,800.00	27.00	6/9/2004
Upper Cuyahoga River Project Area	OH	50,000.00	53,250.00	0.00	0.00	53,250.00	103,250.00	75.00	6/9/2004
West Tennessee Migratory Bird Conservation Area	TN	50,000.00	114,500.00	0.00	2,382,000.00	2,496,500.00	2,546,500.00	2,368.50	6/9/2004
Willow Creek Wetlands Enhancement Project	CA	18,735.00	18,800.00	0.00	0.00	18,800.00	37,535.00	5,000.00	6/9/2004
Number of Projects: 38		1,620,088.20	7,927,543.32	408,600.00	2,492,642.00	10,828,785.32	12,448,873.52	14,464.38	

Canadian Wetlands Conservation Proposals Approved by the Migratory Bird Conservation Commission For Fiscal Year 2005

Table Four

Project Name	Province	NAWCA Grant ($)	Non-Fed $ Match	Non-Fed Non-Match $	Total Partners	Total $ Cost	Total Acres	MBCC Approval
ALBERTA CRITICAL WETLAND & UPLAND HABITAT	AB	220,880	220,880	595,000	815,880	1,036,760	3,790	6/21/05
ALBERTA HABITAT PROGRAM	AB,BC	3,701,015	3,701,015.00	1,009,800	4,710,815	8,411,830	14,277	6/21/05
ALBERTA HABITAT PROGRAM	AB,BC	1,835,688	1,835,688	605,900	2,441,588	4,277,276	8,086	9/8/04
ATLANTIC CANADA WETLANDS CONSERVATION	NB,NS,PE	535,500.00	$535,500.00	$55,250	590,750	1,126,250	1,370	6/21/05
CONSERVATION OF CRITICAL WETLANDS & ASSOCIATED UPLAND HABITATS	BC	842,959	842,959	896,750	1,739,709	2,582,668	1,495	6/21/05
CONSERVING MIGRATORY WATERFOWL HABITATS IN COASTAL & INTERMOUNTAIN BC	AB,BC	674,722	674,722	799,000	1,473,722	2,148,444	1,096	6/21/05
GREAT LAKES WETLAND HABITAT CONSERVATION PROJECT	ON	180,720	180,720	161,500	342,220	522,940	265	6/21/05
IMPORTANT COASTAL WETLANDS IN BRITISH COLUMBIA	BC	357,601	357,601	435,750	793,351	1,150,952	590	9/8/04
MANITOBA PRAIRIE PARKLAND PROGRAM	MB	1,650,966	1,650,966	190,400	1,841,366	3,492,332	18,323	6/21/05
MANITOBA PRAIRIE PARKLAND PROGRAM	MB	917,844	917,844	83,000	1,000,844	1,918,688	25,267	9/8/04
NEW BRUNSWICK WETLANDS CONSERVATION	NB	101,260	101,260	0	101,260	202,520	473	9/8/04
NEWFOUNDLAND & LABRADOR COASTAL & INLAND FRESHWATER WETLANDS	NF	30,295	30,295	0	30,295	60,590	615	9/8/04
NOVA SCOTIA COASTAL & INLAND WETLANDS	NS	70,550	70,550	52,290	122,840	193,390	690	9/8/04
NS, NB & PEI WETLAND & COASTAL HABITAT SECUREMENT	NB,NS,PE	297,184	297,184	148,750	445,934	743,118	760	6/21/05
ONTARIO PROJECT	ON	1,021,700	1,021,700	317,050	1,338,750	2,360,450	2,510	6/21/05
ONTARIO PROJECT	ON	286,350	286,350	132,800	419,150	705,500	945	9/8/04
ONTARIO WETLAND HABITAT FUND PROGRAM	ON	219,950	219,950.00	687,157	907,107	1,127,057	6,000	9/8/04
POTHOLES PLUS PROJECT	MB	523,438	523,438	476,000	999,438	1,522,876	5,870	6/21/05
POTHOLES PLUS PROJECT	MB	523,357	523,357	464,800	988,157	1,511,514	5,865	9/8/04
PRINCE EDWARD ISLAND WETLANDS IN THE AGRICULTURAL LANDSCAPE	PE	50,630	50,630	0	50,630	101,260	150	9/8/04
QUEBEC - PROTECTING WETLAND & UPLAND HABITAT	QC	361,440	361,440	994,500	1,355,940	1,717,380	2,248	6/21/05
QUEBEC / ST. LAWRENCE WATERSHED	QC	510,850	510,850	255,000	765,850	1,276,700	1,172	6/21/05
QUEBEC / ST. LAWRENCE WATERSHED	QC	253,150	253,150	186,750	439,900	693,050	1,388	9/8/04
SASKATCHEWAN HABITAT PROGRAM	SK	3,701,432	3,701,432	433,500	4,134,982	7,836,364	21,114	6/21/05
SASKATCHEWAN HABITAT PROGRAM	SK	1,769,288	1,769,288	128,650	1,897,938	3,667,226	2,035	9/8/04
SASKATCHEWAN PRAIRIE SHORES PROJECT	SK	66,400	66,400	249,000	315,400	381,800	1,540	9/8/04
WESTERN BOREAL FOREST PROGRAM	AB,BC,MB,NT,SK,YT	272,165	272,165	230,240	502,405	774,570	300,000	6/21/05
Number of Projects: 27		20,977,334	20,977,334	9,588,837	30,566,171	51,543,505	427,934	

51

Mexican Wetlands Conservation Proposals Approved by the Migratory Bird Conservation Commission For Fiscal Year 2005

Table Five

Project Name	State	NAWCA Grant ($)	Non-Fed $ Match	$ Total Partners	Total $ Cost	Total Acres	MBCC Approval
CONSERVATION ACTIONS AT THE ALVARADO WETLANDS ON THE COAST OF VERACRUZ II	VER	268,543.00	269,468.98	269,468.98	538,011.98	0.00	3/16/05
EJIDO SAN CRISANTO SUSTAINABLE DEVELOPMENT TRAINING III	YUC	117,640.00	233,089.00	233,089.00	350,729.00	7.41	3/16/05
ENVIRONMENTAL EDUCATION MATERIALS REVIEW	MEX	11,769.00	11,769.00	11,769.00	23,538.00	0.00	3/16/05
IMPLEMENTATION OF LEGAL PRIVATE CONS. TOOLS FOR NW MEXICO WETLANDS	BCS,SIN	162,081.00	165,588.00	165,588.00	327,669.00	10,000.00	3/16/05
LA NACHA LAGOON	TAMPS	92,524.00	98,334.00	98,334.00	190,858.00	0.00	3/16/05
LAKE CUITZEO	GTO,MICH	190,171.00	220,969.68	220,969.68	411,140.68	0.00	3/16/05
MARISMAS NACIONALES (REGIONAL ALLIANCE)	NAY,SIN	50,000.00	132,000.00	132,000.00	182,000.00	0.00	3/16/05
MARISMAS NACIONALES II	NAY,SIN	100,180.00	150,000.00	150,000.00	250,180.00	0.00	3/16/05
MUSCOVY DUCK	CAM,YUC	38,777.00	133,350.00	133,350.00	172,127.00	123.50	3/16/05
RIO GRANDE DELTA	TAMPS	259,343.00	346,546.00	346,546.00	605,889.00	3,900.00	3/16/05
SAN ISIDRO LAGOON	TAB	182,996.00	256,511.00	256,511.00	439,507.00	24,700.00	3/16/05
SANTA MARIA BAY	SIN	238,149.00	462,718.00	462,718.00	700,867.00	7,410.00	3/16/05
THE 2006 - 2007 VERACRUZ MODEL	BCS,TAB	140,000.00	362,000.00	362,000.00	502,000.00	0.00	3/16/05
TIDAL FLOW ENHANCEMENT ON THE RIA CELESTUN	YUC	355,584.00	557,102.00	557,102.00	912,686.00	201,261.35	3/16/05
WATER ACQUISITION IN THE COLORADO RIVER DELTA	BCN,SON	177,400.00	231,700.00	231,700.00	409,100.00	3,803.80	3/16/05
Number of Projects: 15		2,385,157.00	3,631,145.66	3,631,145.66	6,016,302.66	251,206.06